The Father Says Today
One Year of Daily Prophetic Words

Russell E. Walden

DEDICATION

This book is dedicated to my wife Kitty. Without you this book would not have been written.

ACKNOWLEDGEMENTS

Special thanks to my editor Sheryl Was. Your love, devotion and tireless labor are appreciated more than I can express.

Introduction

In 2007 Prophets Russ and Kitty Walden launched Father's Heart Ministry with a view to bringing the voice of the Father to an orphaned generation. God has a voice. He will not leave you without encouragement for your life. Father's Heart Ministry is the culmination of a lifetime of prophetic and pastoral service to the body of Christ by Russ and Kitty. For over 30 years Russ and Kitty have flowed in prophetic gifting and personal prophesy. They have prophesied to thousands who sought them out in hopes of hearing the heart of God for their lives.

Russ and Kitty are committed to the reality of God's voice in the lives of everyday people. They firmly believe that God has a great plan for your life and that no one is disposable. Everyone counts, and it is never too late (no matter what the circumstances) for a new beginning.

In these pages you will find 365 prophetic words birthed in the early hours of the morning over the course of a year as Russ sought out the Father's voice to liberate and empower you to overcome in the face of life's challenges. In I Cor. 14:2 it tells us that prophecy is for "edification, exhortation, and comfort" and not repudiation, rebuke, or denunciation. The unconditional love of the Father is always the character demonstrated by an uncontaminated prophetic gift.

We encourage you to turn to the page corresponding to the day's date and see what the Father would say to assist and comfort you today. It is by no mistake that this is the day and hour that this volume found its way into your hands.

January 1st

The Father says, My voice is the voice that speaks to you in the silence between your own thoughts. My voice is the resonant influence that causes you to tremble in the depths of your being in anticipation of My glory. The ache in your heart expresses the dimension of My passion for more of you that you might have more of Me. That ache is prophetic, says the Father. That yearning inside of you is a prophecy of what I have in store for you in this season.

Come unto Me, My beloved. Let us take our fill of love. Let the bride hear the voice of the bridegroom, and let them enter into their nuptial celebration. It is My breath on the nape of your spirit that is causing your heart to wildly hope against hope that you might break through the mundane desperation of life and experience the miraculous and urgent "now" of My love for you.

It is a new day, says the Father. It is a new hour, and I am bringing you into an intimacy with Me that will plumb the depths of your capacity to love and be loved. I am shaping and molding you to express and portray that love that I might bring you into that which never fails and never falters. Trust My love in this season. Yearn for who I am and what I have promised for you will not be disappointed on a single score.

January 2nd

The Father says today, "No retreat, no surrender!" There can be no compromise with the enemy of your soul in the name of peace. The concessions you make to the enemy in regard to what you now face will only be the starting place of the dark one's encroachment in your life. As with Moses of old, you must come out of enslavement and leave nothing behind. You must come out with your goods, your little ones, and all that you have.

The Cross paid for redemption in your life at every level. You must lay claim to what the Cross provides, or there will be no victory. The blood of Christ bought your freedom, your provision, and your complete deliverance. It also paid for your household and your loved ones. Stand boldly, says the Father, and expect every area of your life to experience that blood-bought provision.

The challenge ahead is nothing to Me, says the Father. Trust in My sufficiency. Allow no doubt to linger in your mind. Anticipate that now (as in times past) I will make good on My Word. Fear not! Fret not! Make your plans in expectation of My Word to be true at every level. I am the Lord your God. Is there anything too hard for Me? Go out now, and in your situation do what I would do if I were in your position for I am in you to will and to do My good pleasure even in this hour and in this season.

January 3rd

I am not capable of unfaithfulness, says the Father. It is not possible for Me to stand idly by while you suffer and struggle. Trust in My voice in your life. Trust in the immediacy of My hand to deliver. Trust, says the Father. Trust who I am and what I can do in your life. My patience is from everlasting to everlasting, and My mercies are renewed every morning.

I never roll My eyes and exclaim, "Oh it's you again. What do you want?" I never tire of hearing your prayers, and I never fail to answer with haste and with joy. That is the nature of My Kingdom, and it is My Kingdom that even today will be made manifest in your life and situation.

January 4th

The Father says today, I am lifting a great weight off of you. They claimed that I placed it there, but that was a lie. You have labored, and you have toiled. However, that time is over for I am coming through for you in this hour. I am going to do for you what you have not been able to do for yourself. Look in the mirror, says the Father, and declare, "No more!"

The angelic assistance has been requisitioned from the heavens, and you will feel their activity in your life before you see it. They are targeting the illegitimate authorities in your life. Those contaminating influences are being broken by the power of the Blood, says the Father. My life is coursing down the avenues of your present and penetrating even into your past. I am performing a great undoing of things you thought could never be resolved. Your eyes will see it, and your heart will rejoice.

You are going to taste and see that I am the Lord your God for whom nothing is impossible and no barrier is impenetrable. I will not be shut out, and I will not be denied, says the Father. I am causing your most caustic critics to make peace with you.

Are you ready to start smiling again? Trust Me, says the Father. The time is now, the change is immediate, and the rejoicing is yours to trumpet to the heavens.

January 5th

The linkage between your present and your past is being broken, says the Father. Your past will not dictate your future. Set your attention upon the "now" that I am apportioning to you. In this season your "now" is a threshold of hope attended by angel porters assigned to usher you into a life worth living. Sorrow and sighing will flee away, and disappointment will now be in your rear view mirror. Surely in life there are challenges, but My anointing on you and My Spirit in you are bringing you to a new authority and new position of trust.

You are going to be taking greater risks in the near future, says the Father. The "you" of yesterday would be incapable of walking in the steps of who I am in you today. Change is upon you, and My call to your deep is a call to cooperation with what I am doing and obedience to what I am saying. Change is not change until it is change, says the Father. I have done My part. Now it is your portion to cooperate with what I have done. You know what I have called you to do; now delay no longer. It is your hour, and iron is hot in the smithy. Strike now, and step into your now.

January 6th

I am going to divide between the light and the darkness in your life, says the Father. I am going to cause you to stand apart from the mixture that has evidenced itself in your life. My righteousness in your life will cause you to shine forth as the sun. Who I am in you will shine so brightly that the enemy will be blinded and unable to plan his next move. My armor upon you is an armor of light, says the Father. I will clothe you with Myself as with a garment of warmth and protection. You will no longer feel naked against the raw elements of life for I will envelope you with My Spirit.

Take your refuge in Me this day. The overflowing scourge will pass by, and you will be unscathed. Not even the smell of smoke will stain you for I am your stay and your high tower of protection. Trust in My provision and My strength, and lean not to the arm of flesh or any false security. When all other resources are expended and fail, you may yet take your comfort in My everlasting embrace.

January 7th

The Father says today that I am raising you up to be a "fearless altar builder." I am commissioning you and assigning you to raise up a pillar of worship in the very teeth of the enemy who seeks to assault you. I am putting a horn of oil in your hand to pour out upon the stones of your consecration to Me. I am going to answer that consecration by fire. The passion of My Spirit burns hot, says the Father, and I will consume the altar that you build Me and render it into a column of fire that will summon the angelic hosts to witness its burning.

You will not be alone in this hour or this season. There are more that be with you than be against you. I am placing within you a Holy contempt for the insults of the enemy against your faith. There will be those who misinterpret your faith and say that you need to be humble. There will be those who think you are provoking a battle that you cannot possibly win. But they do not see the reinforcements I have sent you. They do not see the cloud by day and fire by night. They have not tasted the manna every morning or drunk the water from the rock.

The Father says, "Rejoice!" Let your voice be a trumpet of wrath and your hands beat a "drum of war" for the turbulence you are facing is not a small skirmish but a victory-acquiring war! I am your assurance in this day, says the Father. Let the stones of your consecration be laid in order upon the ground of battle, and let the oil I have put in your heart be poured out with your life as a drink offering of service and love. The battle is yours, the victory is yours, the outcome is assured, and the testimony, says your God, will be great!

January 8th

I said that I would come suddenly to My temple, says the Father. You are the temple I spoke of, and your body is the temple in which I dwell. I will inhabit you with My suddenness. You are going to hear what "sudden" sounds like, says the Father. It is going to get loud around you. You are going to hear My sound, and you are going to feel My wind. Your spirit will be like a sail raised up in a sudden wind (even the wind of My coming), and you will mount up and take flight on the currents of change and deliverance.

You have sought Me for change and asked Me for change. When the angel of change comes, change is the resulting condition in answer to your prayer--change of circumstances, change of fortunes, change of attitude, and change of scenery. No more going around in circles, says the Father, but get ready to cope with the unfamiliar. Do not be alarmed with the view of change. You do not quite know where you are going or what is going on around you. I will instruct you, and I will inform you along the way.

The angel of change comes to initiate the change, and you will feel the difference and know the trembling that accompanies My presence. It is not going to be "business as usual" any longer, says the Father. Get ready to leave something behind, and be prepared to press on to new assignments in My Kingdom.

January 9th

Do you know what I appreciate about you, says the Father today? I appreciate the fact that you have hidden "yes" in your heart when the circumstances of life said "no." You cling to the "yea and amen," and you have not allowed bitterness or unbelief to rob you of your joy. I love that about you.

Heaven's eyes are upon you today. Be not discouraged nor dismayed. Heaven has taken notice that you (even yet) hope against hope and believe against all notions of unbelief that you can have your promise. The Father says, yes! That is My child believing like that! That is My child speaking to the mountain saying, "Be removed!" You make Me a doting Father, and I am rushing to you with the training wheels of faith to make sure you do not falter or fail in the venture of confidence you have embarked upon.

You make a Daddy proud, says the Father. Good job!

January 10th

I love to see the look on the enemy's face when he realizes you are not buying what he is selling. He wants to burden and bind you, but you have chosen to soar. He wants you earthbound and discouraged, but you have chosen to mount up to the heavens. He wants you to think in terms of limitation and lack, but you have only considered My limitless promise.

You are growing, says the Father. Do not stop now. Do not allow yourself to consider what cannot be done or what the circumstance would dictate. My promises in your life set the precondition for victory. My love for you is the determining factor. Never allow yourself to feel like you have to perform or earn what I have freely given. The approbation of heaven is upon you, and I have determined to reproduce Myself in you.

How many times have I proven Myself faithful? I will be found faithful once again. I will deliver and guide and assist you through the current challenge. I am God over the storm, says the Father. I will bring the enemy and all his minions under your feet. I will put your foot in the neck of the one who would rob and steal and kill you. You will know My triumph, says the Father. It was secured 2000 years ago at Calvary.

January 11th

You have asked Me to do some things, says the Father. You have asked, and you have petitioned. You have declared, and you have decreed. I am coming beside you to bring about those things that you have cried out for and desired. Know, says the Father, that by bringing about the things you have desired it is necessary that you enter into the process. I do not answer prayer in front of an audience. The Kingdom of God never comes when you are a mere observer to the process. Enter into the means and methods by which I do the very thing that you have cried out for Me to do, says the Father.

You have wondered at times why you cried out and My response was to give you a task or something to do. It is because I am "the One that comes along side." When I sent the Disciples out into the world, I went with them confirming the Word with signs following. There was a part they had to play and a role I then fulfilled as well. Do you know what it is I would have you do?

As you go out into the world today, My instruction is that you do for others (those you meet along the way) what they cannot do for themselves. What you make happen for others, I will make happen for you. I am going to give you an opportunity to be an agent of breakthrough for others. As you provide for others out of the inventory of your glory, I will provide for you out of the inventory of My glory. That is how things work in My world, says the Father.

The church has missed this concept for centuries and languished in a theology of unbelief and suffering. I place no premium on suffering; but, I am not going to answer prayers on the terms of human demand. At times you feel you are at the end of your tether, and that is true. I allow you to come to the end of yourself so you can dive into who I am and enter into what I am doing. Hesitate no longer. The hour is at hand, and deliverance is near. Open your hand, and open your heart. I will show you where and who to pour your life out to as a drink offering. As you become a spiritual drink and refreshing to others, I will fill your life and moisten you with every good blessing that My treasuries afford.

January 12th

I have called you to live out of your spirit and not your head, says the Father. As you follow Me and respond to My voice, your mind will object because it does not want to be clueless. The questioning you experience is symptomatic of being plugged into My mind and My Spirit, and the natural mind complains because it expects to be consulted and informed at every turn. But, the hour has come that you are walking off the map of human rationale and reason, says the Father. I have not called you to be reasonable or to walk in normality.

If you are going to walk in the miraculous, you are going to have to be more connected to My voice than you are your own human understanding. Marvel not if you find yourself without a clue as to what is coming next. You are learning to navigate in anticipation of the miraculous. I will protect you, and I will breathe My mind upon your mind in a supernatural way. You will begin to think like I think and act like I would have you to act.

This is what a surrendered life must endure to follow Me and know My watermark in your life. It is a good thing, says the Father. It is what you have been praying. This is the rest, this is the refreshing, and now (in this season) is when you will begin to take notice of it more and more in your life.

January 13th

I have heard what your mouth prayed. Sometimes what the heart cries and what the mind interprets are two different things. Would you rather I answer the cry of your heart or the objections of the mind? Let your confidence be in My ability to mold and shape and bring about My goodness in the land of the living. Blessed are the flexible, says the Father, for they will endure to the finish line.

I am endowing you this day with grace to endure and flexibility to trust Me beyond all human capacity to trust. Rest in your waiting upon Me to do that thing that you have asked Me to do.

January 14th

Did I not say in My Word that hypocrisy and being lukewarm were nauseating to Me? It does not offend My character when you hate evil with a perfect hatred. It does not grieve My Spirit when you do not want to keep company with loathsomeness and religious foolishness. If I do not frequent those places, why would I hold it against you if you choose not to as well? Yet, I will not leave you isolated or without the love of brothers and sisters who care about you and those whose hearts burn white hot with passion for My presence.

I set the solitary in families, says the Father. Yes, I have surrounded you with unique and unusual people. They are eclectic in their tastes and even downright strange at times. Is it not nice to not be bored to tears anymore? I told you it would be an adventure when you chose My Kingdom over vain religion. I will vanguard your heart and protect you. It is not the last time you are going to be disappointed. It is time to grow up, says the Father. You are no longer a babe swaddled in the pews of an infant's understanding of spiritual things. Stand up. Stand upright on your feet, and I will gird you with the armor of a battle-ready soldier.

I am giving you the chance to make a difference and fulfill your destiny, says the Father. You get to take some friends and loved ones with you. You are going to have to share with them the things I share with you and talk to them the way I speak to you. No more religious platitudes that never make any impact on the struggles of life. Tell it like it is. Say what you have seen and heard. Share with others what has made a difference in your life, and do not sugar coat it or try to make it palatable to someone's religious thinking. They will thank you for it, says the Father. It is time to be honest, truthful, and loving to My kids.

January 15th

There are relationships in your life that are natural and convenient, but they do not serve My purpose, says the Father. I have indeed called you to be a life poured out to Me in service and in love even to those who do not know Me or acknowledge My love. Love them on My terms for you cannot love them on their terms. They will attempt to dictate to you the preconditions of what they think love is, but I am calling upon you to "do what you see the Father do" and not what they require.

Remember that love is who I am and not merely what I do. Love unconditionally. Lavish My love upon the unlovable. Be liberal in your love with a generous heart and willing spirit. I will open your mouth, says the Father, where the law of kindness will be found. I will even open your hand to the heartless, and your hand will not be found empty. I will demonstrate in you and through you the sacrificial love that contradicts every preconceived idea they have about who I am and what I am all about, says the Father, for they think they understand Me--they have me all wrong.

Many will simply turn and rend you and attempt to take you for a prey. I will instruct you in that moment what to do and what to say. Those who seek to merchandise you will experience the woodshed of God for I am not done with them. Though they think I will let them get away with their mistreatment of you, I will not! So, let your love be in those words and actions that are breathed by My Spirit and not the blind principles of a perverted Christian conscience. I am arising in this hour to manifest My awe and My power, and My fear will come upon many as you hearken to My voice and do the things I instruct you to do and say--those things I instruct you to say on a moment-by-moment basis.

January 16th

Not all meltdowns are negative, says the Father. Do I not say in My Word that I am a fire from My loins upward and from My loins downward? I am raising the temperature of My Spirit in your life. I am burning out all things in your life that offend My blessing upon you. I do not expect you to be a self-starter, says the Father. I am the ignition source of your passion for the Kingdom and the ignition source of your longing for intimacy with Me.

Greater intimacy is possible, says the Father, and greater intimacy is available. You have looked into the mirror of your soul and despised the tepid response you have found there to who I am and what I am doing in your life. I am pleased with that, and I am sending My grace and My fire to heat things up and relieve you of being lukewarm (which has plagued you at times). Yes, there is going to be a meltdown, says the Father. There is going to be a meltdown of things that you will rejoice to be rid of that have hindered you and grieved you as you sought to know Me deeper and be filled with My Spirit.

Receive the burning when it comes. Do not think of it as strange or some negative thing. Not all meltdowns are negative. Not all fires are destructive. In fact, when you have prayed with groanings that cannot be articulated, this is what you are praying for, and I am the God who is answering—yes, I am the God who is answering by fire!

January 17th

The Father says today that My Kingdom is breaching all containment in this hour. The cultural barriers and boundaries man has defined to shut Me out are not adequate to stifle what I am about to do. The lines are being blurred, and it is going to seem chaotic at times. You are going to color outside the lines and operate outside the box religious minds would build around My purposes. I am calling upon you to trust Me and follow the wooing of My Spirit as I use you to speak to the nations.

They are going to demand of you, "What is your authority?" You will answer them with signs, miracles, and wonders. They will ask you, "What would you have me do?" You will teach them the law of the love that never fails. They will ask you, "Is this the time of the end?" You will answer them, "Bah ha ha !" You will laugh, says the Father, and heaven will laugh with you.

You will laugh, and the vanity and derision that men have held Me in will flee away as they are met with the reality of the "Living" God. I will demonstrate Myself alive in you in this hour and cause it to be known that there is a Kingdom in the earth to be reckoned with and a King who will not be denied His due.

This is My plan, and it is your privilege to participate in My purpose, says the Father. Those who were bidden to this task would not come, but I knew you would come. Gird yourself with the demonstration of My Spirit, and prepare yourself with the preparations of the heart that are in man that I have placed in you by My Spirit. You have asked to come off the sidelines, says the Father, and now is your chance. Now is your time to make a difference.

January 18th

The Father says today that My love is reaching critical mass on the inside of you. It is spilling out of your life and bringing fundamental change. Those that have tried your patience and frustrated My grace in your heart are going to be seen in a whole new light. My love, says the Father, is releasing a greater yield of power and faith and joy than you have seen yet. Those that have taunted you and delighted to gore you with unkindness are not going to affect you in this season as they have in times past.

My character is beginning to bear fruit in your character, says the Father. I am going to cause all that is within you to rejoice and to show forth the love that never fails. The enemy cannot stand this, and he will attempt to drag you back to a place of living out of your humanity. The dark one knows that the tide of My love in the earth is changing My people. He knows this, and he fears this change. My love in your life and My love showing forth out of you even toward the unlovely becomes a persuasive force that convinces the most brittle skeptic to know that I am and that I will reward those who diligently seek Me.

Persevere in My love this day, says the Father. As you persevere in love, you persevere in Me because love is not just what I do--it is who I am. As you yield to love, you are yielding to Me. As you walk in love, you are walking with Me (even as Adam did) in the cool of the day. My love is that which will draw you and direct you behind the veil of the natural and cause you to rule and reign in the realm of the supernatural as never before. This is your portion, and this is your inheritance this day.

January 19th

You are not the only one to hear My voice speaking to you, says the Father. There are those around you who sense My approbation over your life but do not understand what it means. Some will say it thundered. Others will say it was angelic activity. But, the Father says, My voice is descending upon you. I am thundering down upon you. I am bringing a detonation of My power and My grace over your life at this hour.

Do not put off the things that are stirring in your heart. Today is the day that I will act and make My arm bare in your behalf. Your faith is causing My grace to explode in your life with a violent release of power. Make way, says the Father. Cast up, says the Father. The mountains of adversity will be removed. Expect it, anticipate it, and plan for it.

Did I not have Noah build an ark for what had never occurred on the earth? Even so, I am calling upon you to erect a canopy of worship that is a response to My promise and not just My performance. Let your praise be focused on what I have promised to do in your life and not just what I have done. Others will look upon your actions and say you have lost your mind. You have simply tapped into My mind, says the Father, and clothed yourself with the expectation of who and what I am prepared to be in your life.

Rejoice, says the Father. This is the hour of promise and the day of thundering down the purpose and provision and protection of My Kingdom in your life.

January 20th

I am bringing fundamental change to your life in this season, says the Father. Did I not say the elements would melt with fervent heat? The fire of My presence is changing and rearranging things within the realm of your experience. The year 2012 is a year of resetting and new beginnings. Those who do not invite change are going to tremble and say, "The sky is falling, the sky is falling." But I say to you the sky is not falling and neither is the earth passing away. Rather, says the Father, My Kingdom is coming in power to turn aright those things in your life that have not served My purpose but have only impeded My blessing and clouded My purpose in your vision.

Put your trust in Me, says the Father. Change is not harmful--change is beneficial. I am the Lord your God. Is there anything too hard for Me? Is there any obstacle that I cannot move? Is there any heart so hard that I cannot and will not bring the full force of the persuasiveness of My Spirit to bear to bring about repentance and reconciliation? You have a front-row seat to a quantum upheaval in the lives of many of those closest to you and many who have made themselves your enemy. I will cause those who are of the congregation of adversity in your life to come and worship at the feet of the God in you who answers by fire.

The urgency of the hour is one that says now is the time of salvation and now is the hour for your miracle, says the Father, not tomorrow or in some more convenient season. Wait upon Me. Trust Me. The iniquities of those who oppose themselves are coming to the full, and their opportunity to align with My purpose is narrowing to conclusion. I am the Lord your God, and I will be feared, says the Father. I will be feared, but I will yet be merciful and give you grace and peace to be able to cooperate with all I am doing in this hour, in this season, and in this day.

January 21st

You have wondered why My presence seemed so near at times and quite distant at other times. You do understand, says the Father, I will never leave you or forsake you. My grace comes to you in packets of divine energy and information. It flows as a current that is rhythmic and even musical at times. When you enter into worship, those are the seasons when the sound of My Spirit and the sound of your soul resonate together in harmony. Barriers can be shattered at those moments.

I have longed to teach you these things about who I am and how I work in the lives of men. It was necessary, however, that I detach your thinking from the religious machine in order for you to experience the organic nature of My connection with you and presence in you. Did I not say that I am the vine and you are the branches?

I never plant anything in a row, says the Father. Quit expecting Me to assemble your life together like a toy or a tool kit. You are the reflection of My passion, turning back upon itself and embracing itself within you. Let My grace flow to you this day and bring the cleansing and the washing of all care and trouble. I will not allow anyone or anything to harm you. Come, says the Father. Venture away from the familiar and mundane, and I will draw back the curtains of My mysteries to you. This is the day My love for you will take on a whole new dimension of intimacy. Are you ready?

January 22nd

Trust Me for the outcome, says the Father. Trust Me to do those things that you cannot do for yourself. Those things that are beyond you and beyond your power to affect are in My hand. They are not left to chance or to the whim of circumstance. I am orchestrating your life, and there is nothing random taking place.

I have written all your days in My Book, says the Father, even this one. You may feel abandoned at times and left on your own, but nothing can be further from the truth. The narrow perspective with which you experience your life does not always take in what I am doing just beyond your view. Did I not promise that I would do nothing without first revealing it to you? I am not leaving you out. I am not making decisions without consulting you. I am not a capricious God who dangles you over an uncertain destiny without care or concern for how it affects you. That is not who I am, and those who have represented Me in this way do not have any clue to who I am or how much I love you.

I am touched and moved with compassion over the things that weigh upon you. Even today I have prepared an escape and a respite from the burdens that would brutalize your hope. Take your refuge in Me. Forsake the cold comfort of inaccessible understanding for you will never understand many things that you will face in life. Do you want peace, or do you want understanding? You cannot have both. I am your peace. Take your solace in Me until this storm is over.

January 23rd

When the wind of My Spirit blows, says the Father, things get rearranged in your life. I am doing a reorganization of your life. It is not going to look like it has looked in the past, and it is not going to be "business as usual." I am going to clear the path between where you are and where I am. I am going to clear the path by burning and shaking and removing all those things that do not represent My highest and best plans for your life. Change is upon you, so do not get too attached to the current arrangement of things. Fundamental sweeping change is descending upon your life, and it is coming in answer to your prayer.

You are going to be tempted to say, "Lord I know you answer prayer. Could you not answer someone else's sometimes?" You are going to feel the stretching, and you are going to experience the pressure, but it is for your good. When it comes to fruition and fullness, you are going to be glad, and you are going to be thankful.

Trust Me, says the Father. I know more than you, I am bigger than you, and I love you. I will never do anything to hurt you. As you walk with Me, I will continually walk you off the map of your current understanding. It will be scary at times, but it will also be invigorating and quite an adventure. You did not want Me to bore you, did you?

When you feel the most vulnerable and threatened, just laugh and say, "Bah ha ha!" For the Lord your God is coming through for you in a big way. I am making the difference in your life that you always wanted to see happen, and you will survive. There will be loss of nothing that is truly fruitful and necessary to your life.

January 24th

The Father says today that the angel assigned to watch over you in life never takes his eyes off of My face. From My face your angel draws the grace and power and love from My heart and transmits it into your life to assist and defend you. Your angel was created and trained to perform this mission with unswerving commitment. Men have not greatly understood the role of the angelic, says the Father. The activity of the angelic is a continual, ongoing presence in your life.

The angels are conduits of grace and power between heaven and earth. They keep the heavens open between you and My throne. They war against demonic interference that becomes heavy over you at times. Your prayers and worship toward My throne provide the platform that angels work from to protect you and minister to you. When you are distracted or diverted by the enemy, they are hindered and delayed in bringing you the resources by My hand from the throne to which you have prayed.

Be diligent in your prayers, and watch for the enemy this day that would draw your attention away from what I am doing in your life. The enemy wants you to give heed to the activities of demonic powers and principalities. Set your focus upon Me. You are where your attention takes you. Even as the battle waxes hot and intense, know that I am with you and that heaven's resources are being made available to you to overcome the enemy in every area of life.

January 25th

The Father says today that you are a part of an Enoch generation. Walking with Me is not about escape but about promotion. As I move in your life to protect and promote you, I will not allow the enemy of your soul to overrun your life. Let your attention be upon your relationship with Me while I contend by My Spirit with the forces of hell that would impede and molest you.

Because I have set My favor and My blessing upon you, the enemy regards you as a target. There are countless kindnesses I have shown you that you do not even notice because it does not matter what the domain of darkness is planning. It only matters that My government and My Kingdom in your life is on the rise and on the increase.

The Father says to you this day to rise up and take your place by My side as we carry through My purposes to completion and fullness even in this 24-hour period. I have empowered you and clothed you with Myself. I have surrounded you with favor as with a shield. There will even be those who will transact with you without realizing why they are being so kind to you and so favorable. They are, at times, simply being motivated by My Spirit in spite of themselves.

Trust and confidence are bringing reward and recompense to you today, says the Father. You are surrounded by My divine assistance. I am bringing the gavel of divine decree down in your favor, and you will look upon the outcome and be thankful at My goodness and kindness which I have promoted to you this day.

January 26th

I have prepared a place for you, says the Father. here by Me. Others would ostracize you and turn away, but I am including you. In My company and in fellowship with Me, you will find acceptance. I love you because I love you, and I will never stop loving or relating to you. I will never take for granted that which you have committed to Me, and I will never neglect you or trivialize your love for Me.

You are seated with Me in the heavens, and I want you to experience that and know the security of My friendship. Even as you have faith and trust in Me, I will also walk in fidelity with you regarding every one of My good promises. I have been accused of being capricious and unreliable, says the Father. It has been said that "sometimes I do and sometimes I don't." Those who espouse that way of thinking know nothing about My character. My promises are always "yes," and My promises are always "so be it."

I am always working to position you to receive the greatest benefit in the shortest time frame. I am calling upon you today to begin afresh and anew to cooperate with My Spirit as I move you and adjust you and, yes, even correct and discipline you. In man's discipline is shame and hateful spite. In My discipline is breakthrough and blessing. This is the hour of breakthrough for you, says the Father. As you continue to cooperate with Me, I will come through for you in small ways and also in the big things that you have waited on for a long time.

January 27th

Disappointment has left its imprint on your life, says the Father. I am backtracking through your past and filling in all the cracks and crevices of sorrow and hurt. I am filling in all the brokenness with something of Myself. Where there has been the sting of rejection, I am applying the salve of My grace and acceptance. I was there when those monstrous disappointments came, and I took inventory of every effect they had on you both inside and out. I will not leave you in brokenness.

I will not leave you in brokenness, says the Father, and I will not leave you scarred by bitter experience. I am visiting you even in the night seasons and soothing the ravages of time and happenstance. Your youth and your vitality of spirit are being renewed. As with every procedure, it will leave you a little tender in those areas, but that is to be expected. Tenderness is a good thing because it means you can feel again. This is how I fulfill My promise to renew your soul. My mercies are renewed every morning, and I would that you participate in and experience that renewal.

It is a new day, says the Father, and in newness you will walk with Me in grace and healing and recovery.

January 28th

I am on guard over you this day, says the Father. You are going to perceive it as you carry on the mundane activities of life. Just as you sense, at times, the assaults of the enemy even though things look normal, I am allowing you to see and know that I am at work in tangible ways in your situation. The waiting has been long at times; I would not leave you without witness of My faithfulness.

You are not going to be disfigured by the pressures that are assaulting you. Your life is not going to be shaped by this set of circumstances. This thing is going to pass and fade and be forgotten. I am going to move so powerfully against the work of the enemy that it is not even going to be a good testimony—it is going to look so easy. Do not accept the dimensions of the problem as the enemy would exaggerate them. It does not matter what it looks like for I am the God of miracles working behind the scenes to quench the violence of fire just at the moment it seems you will be engulfed.

Be pacified with My faithfulness, says the Father. Draw upon My faithfulness at this time even as a child draws upon its mother's breast and finds hope and solace. I am guarding against what you cannot see happening around you, and I am guiding you past the threats you can see. Listen to My voice, and follow My directions. I will not leave you without guidance. I am installing My mind in your spirit to infallibly guide you.

Say within yourself, "Eyes be open, ears be attentive," for I am attuning you to My Spirit like never before. You will walk on solid ground where others have fallen and been devoured. You are the one I am working with, says the Father, to will and to do My good pleasure.

January 29th

When you are crushed and when your spirit is quenched, I will draw near to you, says the Father. Others may hold themselves aloof from you, but I am near to you in those hurtful moments. I am never at a loss at what to say or how to comfort you. The Comforter is who I am and not just what I do. When the words of the enemy sting and bite at you, I will pour in the balm of My Spirit to cleanse the wound and console you with the fresh wind of My Spirit.

The enemy wants to render you into a broken and dry husk of bitterness. Receive the moistening of My Spirit. Stay pliable in My hands. Relinquish the ache of your heart, and come near to Me in these times. I am the God of all comfort, says the Father. I am He that sustains and consoles you in every circumstance and situation. My promises are sure. My guidance is infallible.

Seek My face this day and know that surely, surely you will see My hand at work to deliver and to save. Be assured this day, says the Father, and reassured that I am with you and working in the midst of the chaos of the moment to bring you to safety in Me.

January 30th

I am feeding you the bread of heaven, says the Father. I am tending to you as a shepherd for I am the pastor of your soul. You are the focus of My attention this day. Though it may seem this way at times, you are not alone nor are you isolated. I have placed you in the flock, and I will bring you into fellowship and a relationship with those that are in your "sheep fold."

The flock of God is more than a weekly gathering or a congregational meeting. I have set you in a tribe, and I will help you find your place in that tribe, says the Father. Did I not say in My Word that it is not good to be alone? Though there are seasons when you walk in solitary places, I will set you in a circle--in a spiritual family. It is more than a building and more than an earthly organization. It is a house of bread where you will find the "manna," the revelation of Myself that will not come across a pulpit but rather as a revelation of who I am in the lives of those peculiar people with whom I have surrounded you.

Take My yoke upon you, and learn of Me. I am more than a history lesson and more than a set of values or moral guidelines. I am bringing you into a relationship with the living Jesus, and you will see Me in yourself and also see Me reflected in the lives of others. I will not bear much resemblance to the god of religious tradition. That will be an education for you at times and a pleasant surprise. You will often say, "I thought that is what you were like, but I was not sure until now."

Your experience in Me is a never-ending but ever-deepening revelation, says the Father. Embrace the process and purpose to remain a learner at all times. Never say to yourself, "I have arrived, and there is little more for Me to learn." I have purposed to fill you with Myself in new and interesting ways. This day you will begin to experience Me as you remain open in your heart to who I really am within you and around you.

January 31st

You are not going to be able to validate My blessings in your life by natural reasoning, says the Father. My blessing over you does not arise from My mind but rather from My heart. My passion for you drives My blessing in your life.

It is My passionate love for you that moved Me to the Cross. It is My passion for you that I carried to the throne. From the throne of heaven, this passion moves Me still on your behalf. The heavens are rent by My passion for you, and the hills will melt and flow down in response to My great love for you.

My hand is not still in your situation, says the Father. I am moving in the circumstances to will and to do My good pleasure. I am a faithful Father, and faithfulness is the bread that I will feed you even in this hour.

February 1ˢᵗ

The Father says today that the ministry of angels is a ministry of divine arrangement of your affairs according to My purpose. They work with your knowledge and without your knowledge to strengthen you and deploy you in accordance with My destiny for your life. When you do not understand and cannot fathom the challenge before you, put your trust in My hand to orchestrate your way and guide you. In this season I am enlarging you and increasing your footsteps before you.

Be enlarged, says the Father. Be increased this day. Receive the increase. Be increased with the increase of God for no weapon formed against you will prosper. Every tongue that rises against you will be extinguished. Even in the very hour that you stand in at this moment, the anointing of increase and greatness is upon you to gather the spoil and mete out My judgments of grace and virtue.

February 2ⁿᵈ

You have rights, says the Father, and, yes, you have options. I will not tell you no, but I will give you the opportunity to forego what you want in preference to My perfect plan for your life. The choices you refrain from now will accord you My favor and My grace in the future.

Do not think in terms of being deprived of your rights, says the Father, for I am not denying you. I am simply giving you the opportunity to serve the interests of My Kingdom in a greater capacity. Have I not said that seeking first My Kingdom will result in those things you decline from being added to you in abundance? I place no premium on want of the good things I promised you in My Word. Hold fast, and trust Me for the outcome as I work to bring about My purpose and establish you in

My honor and favor in the circumstance that tries your patience at this time.

February 3rd

Do not be deceived by the diligent inquiry of the enemy, says the Father. He will show interest. He will display sincerity and sobriety. He will feign favor and indulge your good opinion. But, I will expose the strategy of darkness and reveal the false motives of those seeking entrance to your good counsel.

Listen to My voice, and conduct yourself with wisdom and discretion. I will guide you through the falsehoods of the enemy and secure you from every lie. My truth will outlive the deceit of those that walk in darkness, and when all is said and done, you will be left standing in victory, says the Father.

February 4th

They are going to call you a board-certified lunatic, says the Father. But you go ahead and do the thing I have put it in your heart to do. I have hooked you up to a rationale and a logic that proceeds from the throne and not from the plausibility studies of small-minded men, who have no vision beyond their own greed for dishonest gain.

Even in this season that you find yourself in, I am causing you to excel. When others are in survival mode, I am igniting within you a holy ambition to take the spoil and redeem the prey that the enemy thought he held secure. You are going to be spending his dollars, says the Father; he is not going to steal yours. Get ready for a breakthrough on all fronts. Prepare for a party because celebration is at hand. Others are practicing their funeral dirges, and they will look at you and are unable to comprehend what possesses you to act in such a manner.

I have caused your eyes to see the many that are for you in the fight, says the Father, not the few, the pitiful few that are against you. This is the hour and this is the time that the promise made will be the promise kept in your life.

February 5th

You cannot be a social climber and expect to ascend in Me at the same time, says the Father. My Kingdom does not lend itself well to popularity contests or fashion statements. Acceptance in My counsel is about being a trend setter and not following the trends of the day. Many who look at your life and the decisions you make will say, "If it was me, I wouldn't do it that way." You cannot answer them or concern yourself with their insistence that you defer to their influence.

I have called you to follow My voice, says the Father. This can and will often be a solitary experience. You will look around at times and say, "I wish I had some company in this thing you have called me to do, Father." To that statement I reply that you cannot be on the leading edge of My purposes and expect to find yourself surrounded by a crowd of well-wishers. There are onlookers watching, says the Father. They are in the cloud of witnesses that have gone before you. They are cheering you on from the bleachers of heaven. The stakes are eternal, and the prize before you is an incorruptible crown.

I have called many to step out and boldly lead this day. Only a few have allowed themselves to be chosen. Be faithful to the choosing as well as the calling, says the Father. Look not to the right or to the left. I will show you how to take care of the little details that could impede your progress. I will give you access to the grace that shields you from the emotional fallout of the rejection and derision of those who do not respect you because they do not respect themselves.

You cannot listen to your critics, says the Father. You cannot listen to My voice on the one hand and the voices of the naysayers and adversaries at the same time. Make a choice today to sequester your hearing to My voice alone. It is My voice alone that will make all the difference.

February 6th

The Father says today that in this season My voice is going to provoke the enemy and make you a target of persecution at times. Your security and safety will be in harkening to the guidance by which I will cause you to escape from the assaults planned for you. I will guide you and guard you in this season, says the Father. There will be pressure brought to bear on you to deny My voice and to deny a new-found intimacy with Me.

Those who have counseled you in the past are going to see that you are responding to My voice, says the Father. They are going to conclude that you are mocking their influence and control. Do not attempt to explain yourself or make them understand. Simply follow the counsels I have placed in your heart. When you are not sure, do not consult with those who sit in the seat of the scornful. They mock My Spirit and deny My voice. They have no wisdom that will serve you even though they think they have all the answers.

When you need clarity and confirmation, I will send it to you supernaturally, and you will then know exactly what I would have you do and when to do it. Until then, wait and rest and trust. You have asked for My guidance, and it was actually all around you. I did not just now open My mouth, and I have not been silent. I simply opened your ears to find the direction and the assistance that I was already providing you.

February 7th

I am going to lead you to a place of worship that is uniquely your own, says the Father. Worship is not always a shared experience. Worship is not always for the eyes of others. I am drawing you away in obscurity so that you might experience intimacy with Me that only you can appreciate. I will talk to you in that place, and I will speak mysteries that have been hidden and kept as a treasure to be revealed to those who shut themselves away in the alone place with Me.

You have asked Me for this, and I heard you at the appointed time. You cried out to Me in your heart, "Is this all there is?" You cried out, "Is there not more?" Draw yourself away with Me, says the Father. Make time for Me this day. Do not wait for a convenient moment since the urgent always conspires to deny you a deeper intimacy with Me.

Others around you will not be too keen to hear about your

experiences in that place of drawing away. It is called the secret place--not because I have hidden it but because few care to go there. Draw yourself away with Me, says the Father. Drink of the waters of intimacy that only I can provide you even this day.

February 8ᵗʰ

The Father says today that this is the year of walking off your map. There are things you have anticipated and planned for, says the Father, but I am going to detour you from your expectations into the unknown territory of My Spirit. It will be a time of learning and relinquishing. You will see your enemies perish in the turbulence even as Pharaoh's armies perished in the Red Sea when I caused the people to pass over dry shod.

Behold and wonder at the destruction of the adversary, says the Father. You questioned why their hearts were so hardened against you, but I was the one doing the hardening. Did I not say to Moses that I "hardened Pharaoh's heart" so that he would not let the people go? I am a God that hates captivity. I hate bondage and burden with a perfect hatred. I will not have you bound or captive or enslaved to the agenda of the oppressor. I hardened their hearts so that I could make a public spectacle of their inability to thwart My purposes in your life.

You will not fail, says the Father, because I cannot fail. Let your trust be in Me and not in any human instrumentality. Among other things I am the "Lord thy God," and I am indeed a jealous God. When you cast your eye to the right or the left in the midst of a crisis, my passion burns hot for your attention. Trust Me, says the Father.

I am He who is a fire from His loins upward and His loins downward. I am He whose voice causes the door posts of heaven to smoke with the resonance of My voice. My voice troubles the waters and causes the hills to melt and flow down to the sea. My voice is articulating your name even this day, and My voice is delineating and defining your future and your destiny.

February 9th

The Father says today that when you are mocked and shamefully treated I take it personally. I am capable of anger. Those who trifle with you will be execrated from your life and that without remedy. They thought it a small thing to jest and deride you and make light even of your confidence in Me. I will not endure without end the torment and contempt of those who are allowing the enemy of your soul to use them, says the Father.

Just as you cannot take credit for the good things that happen to others when you pray, there will come an end. Likewise, you cannot take responsibility when the opposite happens. I take no pleasure in the destruction of the wicked, says the Father. I will no longer allow you to live without joy. I will remove the oppressor and send My angel to guide you.

I am defending and protecting you in this season, says the Father. Let your words be few. Let your words be circumspect. The enemy knows his time is short, and he is working to make you sin with your mouth. He would tempt you to foolishly charge Me since he hopes to make you a casualty of the process by which I am exposing and destroying his strategies in your life. This is the time to go low and worship. This is the time to carry out your tasks and live each day in godly fear and shamefacedness before Me.

I resist the proud, says the Father. As you maintain humility and quietness before Me, I will bring you through this season without even the smell of smoke upon you from the burning that will remove the adversary from your midst. Trust Me. Let Me take it from here.

February 10th

The nature of My Spirit is to move, says the Father. Therefore, you should never expect to be stationary for very long. I have called you to be like Me and take on My character, so you will always be on the move. You will never put roots down in the sediments of life and say, "Here I will die."

Did I not say, "He that is born of the Spirit is like the wind that blows, and you hear the sound thereof but cannot tell where it came from or where it is going?" You are going to have to get used to people scratching their heads and saying, "I just don't know where you are coming from." Do not even try to give them an answer, says the Father, for like Abram of old you do not know where you are coming from or where you are going. I will not allow you to live out your life in the context of human understanding or human planning.

You did not want Me to bore you, did you? Embrace the move of My Spirit in your life. When I show up, says the Father, I do not settle things down; I stir things up! Do not expect things to be too tidy in this season because they are not going to be tidy--they are going to be messy. The affairs of your life are not going to align themselves according to some neat or symmetrical structure.

I have heard the word, "alignment" in the streets, says the Father. I delight to take what man has aligned and breathe on it and watch them scramble to realign what I have disheveled. I am the God who never planted anything in a row. I am bringing life and movement and the dance of the breath of My Spirit into your life today. Move with Me, and enjoy the activity and fun we are going to have in this season.

February 11th

It is acceptable to be eager, says the Father. I will not disappoint you, and I will not let you down. Indeed, the Father says to despair not. Be of good comfort for I am causing you to see all my goodness in the land of the living. There is no part of Myself that I am holding back from you and no promise that I have set aside saying, "No, I will not make good on that promise." That is not in My nature for in Christ I gave you all that I could possibly give.

God says, there is no reluctance on My part to heal, to save, and to deliver. Open your heart, and open your mouth. You are going to have to ask Me. What the Cross says "yes" to, I will never say "no." Did you hear what I said? I will never say no when the Cross says yes.

Yes to your healing. I took stripes for your healing.

Yes to your loved ones. I was despised that you might be accepted.

Yes to your relationships. I was rejected that you might be received.

Yes to your provision. I was made poor so that you could be rich.

The Cross is My constant. "Yea and amen" to the entire inventory I have laid up in glory. The glory is not far off--it is in you, and it is accessed through your words of faith and confidence in who I am and what I have done for you already.

Draw on My eternal yes. You have heaven's permission slip, says the Father. My default position is not no but yes! You do not have to overcome My reluctance to move in your life because I do not have any reluctance to move in your life. Go ahead--ask. Ask that your joy might be full. Ask that you might receive. Ask that I might establish the merits of the Cross in your life with regard to eternal and to temporal things that others have ignorantly claimed I do not care about.

February 12th

The Father says, I am changing your perception of My nearness to your life. I am transitioning you from a far-off God mentality to a near-minded mentality. I am near to you, and I am near to your situation. You are going to feel My breath on the nape of your neck. You are going to hear My whisper in your ear. You are going to sense Me when I walk into the room. You are going to wake up, and I am going to be two inches from your face and looking right at you. I am near to you, says the Father.

I will never leave you, and I will never forsake you. I have set My affections upon you. That is how you experience My favor. Set your affections, therefore, upon Me. When you set your affections upon Me, I receive that intimacy with you that is the only dividend that the Cross pays back to the throne. Your affection, your love, and your fidelity are all I stand to gain from the earth, says the Father. Everything else is already mine. When I made you and put you on the earth, I gave you the capacity to bestow or withhold the one thing that I desire much-- your love and fidelity.

I am waiting, says the Father. There are many distractions and diversions that would take your focus from the throne. There are many deceptions and misunderstandings that would cause you to offer Me that which I have no interest. I want one thing, says the Father. I want intimacy with you. All else is religious misdirection.

February 13th

The Father says today, "As you say yes to Me, I will indeed say yes to you." I am the "yea and amen" resource in your life. As you are coming out of ignorance and resistance, I would that you not be confused about what I am asking of you. It is most important that you simply agree with Me today. Take that large question mark over your head, and iron it out into an exclamation point!

Walking in the Kingdom and experiencing the dividends of the Cross begins by agreeing with what you sense Me doing in your life. As you rise and go about your day, let your posture be "yes Lord!" and "Thy Kingdom come!" Let your mouth say, "Be it unto Me according to your Word." When turbulence clouds your vision and you cannot see past the assault of the enemy, let your testimony be "all is well" and "it is well with my soul."

Turn away from the stress and strain of trying to believe, says the Father, and just agree with what you know I have promised. Agree with the implications of the Cross. Say "yes" to breakthrough. Say "yes" to the healing, mending, and restoring work I am doing in your life.

You are going to have many opportunities to cry out, "Lord carest thou not that we perish." Do not give into that, says the Father, because we are way out past that, aren't we? Relax. Trust. Know that I am with you this day, and it is My good pleasure to take your "yes" and My "yea and amen" and mingle them together as a recipe for breakthrough in your life.

February 14th

The Father says today that My love is fail-safe. Walking in love places you above failure and above the deceit of a religious mentality. There is no fear in love because there is no failure in love. When you are exhausted, turn to love. When you are weary, turn to love for love is boundless in its energy. Love is limitless in its enthusiasm. Love is never overwhelmed by anything other than itself.

Love is not just what I do, says the Father. Love is who I am, and it is who I have called you to be. You have asked Me many times, "Who am I?" You are an expression of My love in a finite and human form. You are an object of My inexhaustible passion. You are the recipient of love that cannot be extinguished. Know that I am lavishing My love upon you today. When you are struggling, I am love to you. When you are sleeping, I love you. I have loved you since the foundation of the world, and I am eager to love you into eternity.

Men have painted Me as an aloof and distant creator, but that is not who I am, says the Father. I am the personification of intimacy and passion. Even this day a relationship with you and fellowship with you is the whole reason I created the world. So walk with Me today, and know that you are the beloved. Allow the love that is who I am be the motif that you adorn your life with today.

February 15th

My rule is in you, says the Father. My dominion on the inside of you is a manifestation of love, protection, and preservation. Your prayers, petitions, and declarations are the means by which My rule finds access to your outward life. It begins as a well, but it matures into a river. There is a river of grace and power available, says the Father, to engulf your life and swallow your enemies.

As the horse and the rider were thrown into the sea, so the despotism of sin, suffering, and heartbreak will be swallowed up by My life in you and My love for you. My kingship in you is not about suppression for I am not a hard taskmaster. My anger and My vehemence are against the rulers of darkness and the instruments of oppression who have sought to trifle with you and rob you of your peace.

Let your petitions be heard today, says the Father. Cast forth your declarations of faith upon the waters of life, and know they will return to you in the form of answered prayer. Your prayers are the chariots that the angels mount up against your enemies. This is a day of war. This is a day of declaration. This is not a time to draw back or retire in fear. Move forward, says the Father, for I am moving forward with you to reclaim former victories and lay hold of new territories in your life.

February 16th

The Father says today that you are in a time of crossing over. When the Israelites traversed the Jordan, there were things they took with them and things they left behind. You will not be one to only look over and faintly see what might be, says the Father. You get to be a partaker. You get to be a giant slayer. Cities will lay at your feet as you mount up in conquest in My name.

No longer will the walls of the enemy defy you. Take up the cry of conquest for this is the hour and season when your destiny gains full purchase on the ramparts of possibility. No more sliding back. No more wondering and waiting. The end is indeed near, says the Father. The doom-and-gloom people get things right occasionally. This is the end of defeat, the end of sorrow, the end of promises unrealized, and the end of dreams unfulfilled. Open your mouth wide, and will I not fill it? Have I not certified to you My faithfulness?

The trust I justified in the past will be verified in this season, says the Father. Let your expectations be on heaven's campaign of conquest and not on the threats of an enemy, who knows not My mind or My plan or My favor with vanguards for you even now.

February 17th

I have placed you in this life you are walking, says the Father. I have placed you in your life even as I placed Adam in the garden.

Adam's job was to tend and to keep the territory I had apportioned him. Your job, likewise, is to tend and to keep that which I have given you responsibility.

This day I am calling upon you to take full custody of the influences that cross your borders every day. I am a God who understands territory, and I am calling upon you to get territorial over the ground that represents the resources, time, and people I have connected you to in My Kingdom.

No more yielding to the enemy. No more acquiescing to lack, fear, sickness, rejection, sorrow, or broken-heartedness. I have not called you to be broken by the enemy, says the Father. That is not your destiny or your portion. I have equipped you; I set in store for you an armory of weapons 2000 years ago. This is the day you will throw open the doors of the arsenal and take upon yourself that which I shed human blood to empower you.

Rise up, says the Father. The angelic hosts assigned to you are clapping their swords on their shields in anticipation and eagerness of the fight. They will not move forward unless you are leading in the fray. The enemies of joy can feel the hair standing up on the nape of their necks. They do not see it yet, but they sense their defeat is looming. What are you waiting for? Take your territory! Take the fight to the foe this day, says the Father. This day you will rejoice with your foot in the neck of your enemies and know that the victory I paid for on the Cross is apportioned to you in your circumstance and situation.

February 18th

You have asked Me how to "wait upon the Lord," says the Father. That is a question I am prepared to answer today. "Waiting upon the Lord" is more about what you do not do and why than it is an attitude of rest or passivity. The enemy is looking for a reaction out of you today. The only way the enemy knows you are still in his grip is if you are wriggling in his grasp. Do not give him that privilege.

No matter what storms of emotion and turmoil seize you in your current situation, look in the mirror and declare, "bah ha ha!" Did I not say, "He that sits in the heavens shall laugh?" You are not in the grip of the circumstance this day, says the Father. You are seated with Me in heavenly places far above all the works of darkness.

Learn to live and to navigate the pressures of life without reacting. Do not react with your words or your actions. Wait upon Me. Wait upon My go-ahead to speak. Wait upon My go-ahead to act. Then in your acting and speaking, I will enter in and devastate the plans of the enemy laid against you.

You are an overcomer today, says the Father. Now arise and overcome!

February 19th

The warm approval of heaven is upon you this day, says the Father. There are going to be days like this that heaven smiles upon you. This is one of those days. There are going to be days that the kiss of heaven moistens your brow. This is one of those days.

I am foolishly fond of you, and I do not particularly care what others are complaining about. They are murmuring and bemoaning that they never got treated so well. I am provoking them to jealousy by the goodness I am bestowing upon you even in this hour. The commendation of the Son is affixed to your epaulets, says the Father.

Even this day the salute of the Father is recognizing you. The approval of the Kingdom is in visitation within you, and My approbation is seeking to take up residence upon your life. Ask Me, says the Father. Ask Me, and I will not merely give the half of My Kingdom, but I will bestow upon you a Kingdom wholeness and Kingdom portion that will define and dictate the total annihilation of the works of darkness against you in this season.

February 20th

You are not on 90-day probation, says the Father. I am not sitting back to see how you will work out in this new assignment I have given you. The whole weight of heaven is behind you, and I will not leave you or forsake you. I will not withdraw My support from you, and I will not take My hands off of that which you have applied yourself to accomplish.

Let all timidity and insecurity be lifted up and off of you. Timidity is a disease of spirit that I am healing now in your life at this very moment. You know Me, and I will be known of you further. My deep is calling to your deep. My sound is resonating within you. As the cry of your heart harmonizes with My sound in the heavens, the walls of opposition and resistance in your life will tumble down.

Trust Me, says the Father. The hour has come. The hour is now. Take the spoil and rend the prize from the hand of the enemy. I am with you and in you and making My strength to be your greatness even in this season.

February 21st

I am the God who never planted anything in a row, says the Father. There are things in your life that you thought would come sooner but are going to come later. There are things you thought would come later, but they will come sooner. There is no map for where I am taking you because no one has ever been there before. There is no map--there are only coordinates of intimacy with Me.

As you track the intimacy, I am going to take you deeper in Me. My deep calls to your deep, says the Father. As you read the accounts of those that have gone on before you and get so stirred with their exploits, I am saying to you that they are not the frame of reference for where I am taking you. Every generation has its own unique testimony. You are carrying within you an opportunity to be a catalyst for transformation. You have before you, even now, an opportunity to set the high-water mark for the outpouring of My Kingdom for the next 10 years.

Listen to My voice. Do what I tell you, and go where I send you. I did not set any limits on what was possible; that was done by those who have not entered in and will not let anyone else enter. I am about to shake them, says the Father. I will shake the naysayers and the doom-

and-gloom people, and they are going to get more shrill. They will cry, "The sky is falling," but the sky is not falling—the Kingdom is coming! You get the opportunity to participate in this process as you draw yourself away with Me and hear My voice and respond in haste and in obedience.

February 22nd

The Father says today that failure is not a possibility in your life as long as you are connected to Me. Let your heart be livingly connected to Me today on a moment-by-moment basis. The perils of circumstance and trials will try to capture your attention. Say within your heart, "I only have eyes for you, Lord." Those things that threaten and those storms that are gathering will pass, and you and I will be left standing.

At My breast, says the Father, you will find comfort and rest. I am your Comforter in the rigors of life. I see the suffering and the pain. You mask it so well at times that no other earthly observer would ever know the sorrow of heart that plagues you. I know, says the Father. I know your heart, and I say to you this day that sorrow and sighing shall flee away. They will be replaced with jubilant worship and exalted praise as I come through for you in the very areas of life that you have barely dared to ask of Me.

Be comforted, says the Father. I am wrapping Myself up in you today with all the love and constancy of a devoted Father. You are never too grown up to find your solace in Me.

February 23rd

It is not good to be alone, says the Father. There have been times you have been surrounded by well-wishers but felt completely abandoned. Even in those times I have whispered in your spirit, "I will never leave you; I will never forsake you." But even then, there was a need to look someone in the eye and know they were standing with you no matter what. This is the singular onslaught of hell that My children have succumbed to more than any other. When you are one heart and one soul on the earth, the enemy knows that nothing shall restrain you--even the total destruction of his domain of darkness.

You will not be alone, says the Father. I am positioning those around you who will enter into agreement with you over your vision and even the desires and ache of your heart. They will be as David and Jonathan to you, says the Father, and I will pour in the oil of selflessness that will secure that relationship when the cost becomes great; they are on their way to you even now.

There is one who has been in your life but been overlooked because no one takes them seriously. It is that very one who is going to be your stalwart friend when all others have fled. I am speaking to these Kingdom companions even now as I speak to you. Do you know what I am saying to them? "It is not good to be alone," says the Father.

February 24th

Sometimes you find yourself in an unnecessary crisis, says the Father. Remember Peter when he sank under the waves? People look at that story, and all they see is Peter walking on the water. What I remember was reaching down into the brine and wrapping My arms around him. I remember the smell of fish and fear on his body and his desperate cry, "Master I perish!" I was never more proud of him than at that moment.

The lesson Peter learned was to frame his questions more diligently. When he vaulted over the rail and walked on the water, he ask Me a question to which there was only one answer, "Master, if it's you, bid me come." Well, it was Me after all, so I bade him come to Me knowing he would instantly find himself in an unnecessary crisis.

There have been times you are so anxious to do something in My Kingdom that your attitude is almost, "Lord I'm going to do something. If I do it wrong." For your sake I regret the escapades of presumption, but for My sake I cannot wait to come to your rescue. So, go ahead and ask, says the Father. You cannot disappointment Me, and I will not be angry. There are times when the entire scope of My grace in your life is applied to make you prosper in the midst of a huge mistake. When the religious crowd sees Me do that, it makes them so frustrated. I am going to love you anyway, says the Father, and there is nothing they can do about it.

February 25th

Do you understand, says the Father, how fragile the obstacle is that is in front of you? Do you know how powerful you are and how strongly I am standing beside you? Do you know just how many angels have been assigned to war and minister on your behalf until captivity is held captive on your behalf?

The stockpiles held for you in the heavens are immense. Do you know that you hold the requisition forms to bring heaven to earth? You have manifested heaven before, so what hinders you now? You can do this, says the Father. You can quench the violence of sword, cross the impenetrable barrier, and break down the obstacle that the enemy has erected before you. It is all smoke and mirrors on the enemy's part anyway. The enemy does not have one substantial impediment he can cast in your way because the Cross just blows them all out of the way.

Make your decisions today not on the red light the enemy is giving but the green light I am giving, says the Father. Go forward, and claim your destiny.

February 26th

The prophets speak contrary to one another at times, says the Father. One will prophesy a day of gloom and darkness and another prophesy the morning spread on the mountains. According to where your affections lie, they are both right. Set your affections on Me, says the Father, and you will never be shaken.

What you cling to and what you are willing to relinquish for My will in your life determine the character of your current season. What can man take from you that I cannot replace? What can man threaten that I cannot restore with one act of divine grace?

Mourn not when the prophets portend impending loss, says the Father, for there is nothing hidden in Me that will be molested by that which is coming upon the earth. Your life is mine and all that you possess. I will maintain and sustain you. You will have resources and provisions that others will see and wonder, "How can this be?" Your answer will be to bring them to a loving Father, who cares for the least sparrow that falls from the bough.

February 27th

The Father says today that the processes of your life are My domain. Stop praying the process, and start praying the end result. How I get things done is up to Me and not up to you. Many times your prayers are frustrated because they reflect how you think I am going to do something rather than simply trusting Me for the outcome. Leave the details to Me, says the Father.

Moses had no clue how I was going to get him over the Red Sea. Time and again I totally surprised Elijah with the means by which I delivered him. With just 300 soldiers under his command, Gideon was completely in the dark regarding how I would bring the Midianites to defeat. It would have been a waste of time for them to lay awake conspiring to ask Me to do thus and so when all they had to do was leave the details to Me.

Stop praying out how you think I am going to do the things in your life. The Israelites died in the wilderness because they could not get their eyes off the process and leave the details to Me. Pray the end result instead, and your peace will be greater, and you will enjoy the journey instead of being tormented by unnecessary worry and care. I have this, says the Father. Sit back and enjoy the ride.

February 28th

Have I not said, "Out of the heart are the issues of life," says the Father? Safeguard your heart from the negative! Put a wall of opposition between yourself and the situation, the people, and the environment that continually reeks of the negative, defeatist attitudes of unbelief.

The enemy of your hopes has packaged the negative in such an appealing way that the darkness waltzes in without nary a knock at the door. It is time to ask for your key back! What settles in your heart in abundance will be produced in your life, says the Father. This is the way I designed the human heart to work for you and not against you.

Fill your heart with those things that are pure, and the pure will usurp the impure in your life.

Fill your heart with those things that are lovely, and lovely things will appear on your stoop every morning.

Fill your heart with those things that make a good report, and the good report will find its way to your back door.

Fill your heart with those things that arise from virtue, and My virtue will go forth from My throne and heal your land.

Is there not any praise, or any positive, blissful fact to entertain your thoughts this day? Think on these things today, says the Father, and they will be the predictors of your tomorrow.

February 29th

The Father says today that when Solomon built the temple his purpose was to provide a place for the Ark of My Presence. When I went to the Cross, I was preparing a place for you here by Me. I was making provision that the Ark of My Presence would dwell in you and follow you and rest upon you in all your daily activities and even throughout your life.

As I blessed the house Solomon built, I am blessing the house and the temple that is you. My eyes are open toward you, says the Father. I have set My name within the house that you are because you are the temple not made with hands. My respect is not toward what man might build but toward the temple that was erected in you by the rigors of the Cross. My favor is toward you, says the Father, for you are that dwelling place of which Solomon's house in all its glory was just a shadow.

My covenant with Solomon was to hearken to the prayers made toward that house, and did I not say that you are My house and that the

Kingdom of God is within you? When you cry out to Me, you are calling upon resources and graces that are already stored up within you. The angels of God are descending and ascending night and day upon you. Do not regard My temple lightly, says the Father. Honor that temple, and understand that I am not a far-off God but a near God, who is attendant upon every cry of your heart even this day.

March 1st

My purpose in this moment of your life, says the Father, is that you find your ascension in Me. I have already come to you in full humanity. I expect you now to find in yourself the fullness of My divinity in your heart, in your circumstance, and in your situation. Draw on the finished work. The enemy wants you to think there is something lacking, and that is why your answer is not forthcoming. That is not My truth, says the Father. There is no further action necessary on My part to bring a total and miraculous transformation to your life.

Lay hold to and activate with your words and your actions all that My descent into the human condition afforded. The act of faith and the words of faith I am looking for from you have nothing to do with calling Me down again or raising Me up again or repeating anything I have already fulfilled. Trust in the finished work, says the Father.

The provision of Calvary is an "ascension" provision, says the Father. I am not coming down again (to suffer); you are going to have to come up to Me. I have made provision for you to do exactly that. Come up to Me, and be seated in Me and with Me. From that place you will rule and conquer now. There is no victory or authority in eternity that cannot be accessed by your audacious and boldness of faith for your "now," says the Father.

March 2nd

We are going to be revisiting some prior experiences, says the Father. Today I want to reiterate to you My faithfulness and adjust some drift in your thinking concerning what you think I will and will not do in your life. I made some promises to you in the past. The waiting has been long, and it gets wearisome scanning the horizon for an answer you are not sure you would recognize if it was revealed. Did I not make a sure and certain promise to you, says the Father? Do not make the mistake Abraham made by coming up with a witty means by which the impossible can be worked out on a human level. Do you really want an Ishmael experience?

I said in My Word and I breathed into your heart sometime ago a promise, "You shall not be in want." I am the supplier and the refiner of that promise, says the Father. I am never late, and I never come up short. There is nothing anemic about the answers I am bringing to you. I am going to address the whole package of problems you are facing, and I am going to blast the enemy with one blast of My nostrils. You will remember him no more.

Failure is not a possibility, says the Father. It does not exist in My character or in My Kingdom. I will not fail you, and I will not allow you to fail. You have been here before. Did I not come through back then? Therefore, trust Me now, and move forward for I am behind and beside you. I am before and beyond you. When you show up on the day of battle, you will see I am the one you will find waiting there to deliver on every promise of support and alliance.

March 3rd

I am reproducing My faithfulness in you, says the Father. You will have the opportunity today to demonstrate My confidence and My rest in the midst of conflict and difficulty. Say within yourself, "I will have the faith of God." Be determined, says the Father, and be resolute. You will never be disappointed when you make the assumption that I will come through for you and stand by you when all others falter and flee.

It is not presumption to expect that I will produce a miracle in your life. It is not arrogance to expect My Word and My promises to you to come to pass. Man's idea of humility carries within it a component of unbelief and timidity. That is not what I say is humility, says the Father. True humility is expecting what I say to come to pass no matter what the circumstance indicates or what others think will or will not happen. True humility operates on the assumption that you can do what My words say—that you can do and have what My words say you can have. True humility will never allow the circumstance to contradict what I have promised.

I exalt the humble, and I will deliver the contrite of heart. I am gathering you to My bosom in the high and lofty place where sin cannot stain you and Satan cannot torment. Take your solace in Me, and expect Me to be who I am and do what I can do in your life today.

March 4th

The Father says today that you have been ransomed by the one thing the enemy cannot contaminate in the earth. The blood of Christ is that one thing the enemy, man, or time cannot corrupt. You have the spiritual authority to apply the uncontaminated blood of My humanity to your life. The blood of Christ is available to you, and it is accessible to you through your words. My life is in that blood. My purity, my power, and my provision are in that blood, says the Father.

By intoning with the words of your mouth, "I apply the blood," you are taking something incorruptible and pure into your mouth and sanctifying the very atmosphere around you. My blood changed the heavens when I applied it upon the mercy seat in the throne room. Heaven was forever changed because something holy and at the same time very human had sanctified the altar in heaven. The angels covered their eyes with their wings at that moment. It was the first time they saw something they did not understand and knew they would never understand. They wept and cried, "Holy! Holy! Holy!"

This scene is played out in your life every time you invoke the efficacy of My shed blood, says the Father. The enemy hates the blood because he cannot usurp it or circumvent its power. So open your mouth today, and spiritually apply the blood that was shed for you. Apply it to the doorposts of your heart. Apply it to your lips. Apply it to your home, your loved ones, and all that you possess. Apply the blood, says the Father, and in that moment you will activate heaven on your earth and bring protection and provision and My presence to bear on all that is in you and all that pertains to you.

March 5th

The Father says today that demonic interference will not keep you from hearing My voice and knowing what is on the morrow. I said in My Word that My sheep hear My voice, and they will not follow any other voice. As long as you live out of your sheep nature, you will hear Me with clarity. When your hearing is obstructed, it is not because the enemy has put his fingers in your ear--it is because he has put his thoughts in your mind. Still the questions in your mind, says the Father, and My voice will come through to you in softness and stillness. Be still and know, says the Father. I will calm the mental storm and still the waves of emotion that threaten to swamp you at times. In that stillness My voice will come through without question and without wondering, "Is that you Father?"

I have ordained that you be a hearer, says the Father. I have given you ears to hear. I have given you eyes to see what is going on around you in the eternal realm. Live out of your sheep nature. What does that mean? Live out of your total dependence upon Me for your next breath and for your next decision. Quiet the raging thoughts that drown out all other voices. My voice is the only voice that remains in the quietness that will come to you as you learn to be still. Be still and know, says the Father. Be still this day, and you will come to the intimacy you seek beyond the demands and raging of natural things.

March 6th

The enemy of your soul gravitates to strife and contention. He seeks out the atmosphere where sharp words and harsh glances rule. Above all else in your day, let My peace rule over your disposition and your words. Determine in your heart that love will be the law that you will walk in this day. Love chokes the enemy and stifles his activity and operation in your life. Let My love in your heart find expression in your life over the next many hours for it is crucial for your success in the assignment that this day represents.

Love is a noxious fume in the eyes of the enemy. My love flowing out of you blinds him to what I am doing in your life and puts him on the defensive. You will have opportunities to step out-of-love today. Do not fall for it. Do not allow the unkind actions of others rob you of the authority and supremacy you walk in when you release My love in the situation.

When all other emotions and sentiments falter and fail, love will still be conquering over all. Love is who I am, and it is who I want you to be. Love arises out of My personage, says the Father. I want love to be not merely your conduct but your very person. It will then become effortless and flawless. When you allow love to find expression in your life, you allow Me to ascend over all the strategies of hell. You will then see that miracle you have asked for and hardly dare to believe. It is available on the wings of love.

March 7th

There is a blessing for those that I find alert in the third watch of the night. Be about your Father's business wherever you find it and whenever you are called to it. I will work with you when you work with me to bring Kingdom superintendence over your life and the lives of those I hold you accountable.

Let your mind think my thoughts of those precious charges. Let your mouth pray and speak My words over them in the night. As you declare and decree, so shall I do and accomplish, and none of your words will fall to the ground, says the Father.

March 8th

The Father says, let your joy be full in Me. There is more of Me than you have capacity to enjoy. Revel in who I am on the inside of you. Joyfully deploy who I am by your prayers and by your faith in your life's circumstance today. I will fill your life, fill your need, and fill your expectations exceedingly.

March 9th

The Father says, I created eternity as a measure of the finality of my love. Heaven, earth, and the entire expanse of history and human experience cannot encompass my love or define its boundaries.

I love you. I love you today. Love is who I am and what I do on a consistent basis. Comfort yourself in my love as you go about your day and know it as the protection wrapped around you, protecting and caring for all affairs of your life.

March 10th

The Father says, I am putting the "shiny" back in your life today. If you could get a whiff of your future, you would smell that "new car" smell. As for Me, says the Father, every day when you rise up is like Christmas morning. I want you to be that excited about your life today.

You see, says the Father, I choose not to leave you out or allow you to suffer lack in any way. Just as the shoes of the Israelites did not wear out in the wilderness, I will not wear you out. If I cared about the condition of a pair of shoes, how much more do I care for you?

March 11th

The Father says, you have been born again of a seed that is incorruptible. It proceeded from eternity and was gestated on the Cross and brought to birth when you yielded your life to Me and asked Me into your heart. I have accorded you, oh My child, My irreducible life.

Shall anything, anyone, or any circumstance diminish what the death and resurrection of My Son has brought to substance in you today? Rejoice in that substance. Exalt in who I am in you.

March 12th
The Father says, the earth is shaking and economies are unstable. Societies around the world are in upheaval. Come to Me all you who are weary and heavy laden. I am the haven of unshakable shelter even when friends, family, or the crust of the earth under your feet fail you.

Fear not, says the Father. Do not allow dismay to take hold of you or overwhelm you. I am there in your situation, going before and behind and around you to uphold you and lift you up. Rest yourself in Me today.

March 13th

The Father says, I am not a God who is idle. I am not an absentee Father. I am superintending all the affairs of your life today and sending needed assistance. When you feel estranged from Me or when the intensity of My presence wanes in your life, move closer to Me.

Seek Me in your thoughts. Seek Me in your heart. Seek Me where you find Me in the lives of others. I will be found of them that seek Me. I will kindle the embers of your love for Me and blaze afresh the joy of your salvation.

March 14th

The Father says that it is time to fly. I have stirred your nest. I have made it uncomfortable for you to stay where you are today. The soft down of mother's feathers have been replaced by sharp sticks and twigs. It is time for you to fly.

There is a feast to be found in the "above" realm, says the Father. You will only find the leavings of others where you are now. I did not call you to scratch the ground like a barnyard fowl. You are made for the heights, and it is there I am calling you to soar.

March15th

I am showing up in your life today to make a difference. I did not make the sacrifice of the Cross to maintain a respectful distance from your problem. I am up to my elbows and covered up in what you are going through today, and I am changing things, says the Father.

Look for what I am doing. Applaud what I am doing. Identify what I am doing, and speak to it! Cooperate with it. Let nothing stand in your way of entering into that thing I am doing in your life today to bring you to your destiny.

March 16th

The Father says, time is not at a premium in your life today, but rather time is at your disposal. I created time to be the servant of my children. I put you in your life (even as I put Adam in the garden) to tend, to keep, and to engulf your life with your influence and your vision. Speak to the elements of your life, and command them according to the promises of My Word.

Let your words be stout against the circumstances of your life that contradict My promises to you. I have armed you, and I have equipped you. Open your mouth wide, and I will fill your mouth. Unleash my words, and I will fill your life with the manifest substance of My good promises.

March 17th

No weapon formed against you will prosper. Yes, you have an enemy. Yes, you are on his radar. No, it is not possible that his purposes and plans will win over in the end. Hearken to My voice.

My words are rumbling through you in the night and whispering My purposes to you even in the daytime. I am that voice speaking over your shoulder saying, "This is the way--walk you in it."

March 18th

No more looking downward my son and my daughter. This is the hour for upward focus. You are seated in heavenly places in Christ. No weapon formed against you will prosper. You will condemn every tongue that has risen against you in judgment. I would that you view your life from the "in Christ" perspective because only then do you see with My eyes, think with My mind, and act with My heart.

Have no fear, no trepidation, no hesitation, says the Father. Set your foot forward with purpose, and I will enlarge your steps before you. I will provide for you this day in the land of the living and affirm all my good Word on your behalf. Look up! See what I see, and you will have today what I have--total victory!

March 19th

You are my foundling, says the Father. I am establishing my paternity in you this day. You are no more abandoned. You are no more unknown for you are known to Me and known of Me.

I call you Son. I call you Daughter. Look at your hand, says the Father, and you will see the signet of My favor upon you as you go about your affairs this day. I am sending the angels of My favor to pave the way and go before you. Let your heart cry, "Abba!"

March 20th

It is not a day of leisure, says the Father. It is a day of war. Look! The enemy of your soul is at the gate, and the sword of My Word is in your mouth. Slay the enemy! Open your mouth, and release my blade edge of victory against the one who opposes you. My armaments are on you and about you.

Angelic hosts surround and aid you. The land is yours! Take your territory, and do not be denied. This is the hour, and this is the day of vengeance against the usurper who would steal My blessings from your life. Let your mouth pray. Let your words war this day, says the Fataher, and I will turn back the shadows until victory is brought forth into a manifest substance in your life.

March 21st

I would not that you be a casualty of war, says the Father. The enemy spied you as a resource. He acted that he might consume and destroy you. But I have said you are not disposable. I will not allow the enemy to tread down My treasure, and you are my treasure!

Rejoice, says the Father. Rejoice as one whose warfare is done away with! Hold fast to my pinions, and I will translate you and transport you above the fray to My resting place.

March 22nd

Understand My purposes this day, says the Father, for I would that you open yourself to Me and be pollinated with My purposes. I am sending My prophetic Spirit to bring you sweet pollens from many fields that you might become fruitful and bring forth the nectar of My words for the spiritual geography where you are planted.

Receive the residue that is distilling in your spirit day by day. Hear My words from those I send your way. Tuck them in your heart, and allow them to germinate and grow. The planting that will be produced will save you, says the Father, and it will save others who are crying out for My sustenance.

March 23rd

The Father says, My love is constant in your life. People come, and people go. Times change, and circumstances change. Even this day the landscape of your life is ever-changing. Beneath it all and over-arching the whole is the assurance of My love and My watchfulness over you.

As you go about your activities, I will be there asserting Myself into every exchange and every interaction. Look for Me there. The acknowledgement in your eye that I am present is that which thrills Me beyond words. I love you. My love is the one constant in your life--all other things change. Mourn not for that which passes away and that you thought would be there forever. That is not My plan. As you grow and learn and heal and mend, the wisdom of change will comfort you. It will give you My perspective and lead you to greater dependence on Me for My love never changes.

March 24th

I am upholding the very atoms that comprise your life today. I am even causing the molecules around you to cohere by an active effort of My will. Your efforts to "hold everything together" are utterly futile! It is not up to you, says the Father.

Cast your cares and anxieties upon Me, and know that I am providing necessary superintendence and assistance at every point of pressure in your life. Do you trust Me? Let Me take it from here.

March 25th

The Father says, go ahead and dream. Dream a bigger dream. Dream a dream of conquest and victory for that is the "king" in you rising up to take the dominion paid for on the Cross. When I spoke through My prophet Joel of the outpouring of My Spirit, I did not portend the speaking of tongues of angels, but rather, I spoke of dreams and visions.

I have poured Myself within you that you might be a dreamer and a visionary. Go ahead and dream. Your job is to dream the dream, and My part is to make the dream a reality.

March 26th

What dwelling place will you build Me, the Father asks? You are the only fit dwelling for My glory. Have I not said My glory shall rest within you? Did I not send the apostles, the prophets, and my servants throughout the ages to proclaim the human heart as My chosen habitation?

You are My dwelling place. If you (being but dust) take care of the place where you lay your head, shall I not take care of the resting place of My glory, which you are? Rest in Me today. I will be superintending all your affairs today and sending needed assistance.

March 27th

The Father says, if you want to be "out of the box," you have to go over the top! No longer will you be hemmed in by the opinions of men. Your destiny is not determined by the judgments of others but by My sovereignty. They would put you in a "cardboard box" destiny, but I have set you at My own right hand in heavenly places. Let your ear be deaf to their words and your eyes be open to My vision for you.

I have heard their words, says the Father, and I have said over them, "no more." Look up, and see your way of escape. You have been tempted to believe and accept the limitations others would impose on you. They have not had faith for you because they do not have faith for themselves. The wind of acceleration is blowing and, today is your day! Rise up and escape, leaving the past behind and embracing the future I planned for you since the before the foundation of the world.

March 28th

The Father says, there is no panic button in the Kingdom, My child. This situation did not take Me by surprise, and I am not wringing My hands over what to do. Let your leaning be upon Me and not the arm of flesh. Natural solutions carry with them the seeds of failure. Look! Even now I am causing your feet to rise out of the billowing waves that those looking on think will swallow you up.

You are not going to get swallowed, says the Father. You are no Jonah. Yes, I know they have called you that because they did not understand why you did not run to the fight. The only fight I have called you to is the good fight of faith. Trust Me, says the Father. I have your interests at heart. I have no hidden agenda for your life. My only agenda was made nakedly plain on the Cross. Trust in that and trust in Me. Tomorrow will be a better day for I will be a bigger God day by day as you walk with Me through this time.

March 29th

Your enemies are pouting today, says the Father. They thought they could come and accuse you before My throne. I sent them packing because I am in no mood to hear the charges they want to bring against you. You obeyed Me, says the Father, and in that obedience you angered their religious spirits. Those religious spirits are not accustomed to being denied having their way, so they have camped outside My door expecting that I will hear them on another day.

Take your shelter in Me, says the Father. Take your counsel from My heart for I am sending My voice to you on a wavelength they cannot discern. It is the wavelength of unconditional love. Let your ears be attuned--not to the cacophony of carnal voices but to the ceaseless harmonies of My love that I am sending your way today.

March 30th

The Father says, tone it down My child--tone it down. I am sending a calm to you that will quell any storm (whether the storm is within or without). Have I ever failed you? Have I ever left you without comfort? My Comforter is coming to make known My affection for you.

I am foolishly fond of you, says the Father. Against all the complaints of your elder siblings, be brave, be strong, and be unswerving in your fidelity to Me this day. I will strongly support you with My provision, power, and victory.

March 31st

You are not alone. The angels of God are on assignment, guarding and guiding you in your steps this day. Let your thoughts be upon Me, and let your heart follow the leading of My Spirit. I am rising up to meet you and to carry you through to a place of blessing. Look for divine encounters and "God connections" today.

Your steps are not random, says the Father. Your every footfall is ordered by My hand to advance you in My plan for your life. Rejoice in My meticulous, intimate care for you. Today is a "God day," and as God, I shall be over all your affairs.

April 1st

The Father says, I am making all things new in your life today. Dust off your dancing shoes, tune up your instrument, and open your heart for a fresh wave of joy and gladness. No more will there be sadness and tears and no more waiting in the night for an answer that never seems to come. The angels of God are populating your life "wall to wall" and "floor to ceiling."

Do you not know how much I love you? Do you need a reminder? Look to the Cross, then look to the throne, and then look in your own heart and life. See how this day plays out, and when you lay your head down at night, tell Me if I do not do all things well.

April 2nd

The song in your heart today is as thundering doom in the heart of your enemies. As your heart is lightened, the heart of the enemy of your soul is darkened with gloom. He knows that the joy in your heart is forcing his exit from your situation. Your rejoicing is his funeral dirge. I am enforcing in your life today the defeat I brought on your enemy at the Cross. I have said you shall have joy. I have spoken forth from My heart that you shall have rejoicing.

Open your mouth wide in thanks and praise. Open your mouth in jubilation. Laugh in the face of your enemy this day. No weapon formed against you shall prosper. Every tongue that rises against you in judgment shall be condemned. Hide yourself in Me today. Take your rest under My pinions. Exalt over your enemies from the ramparts of the safety that My presence is affording you, says the Father, for I will allow no man to set on you to hurt you.

April 3rd

The doom-sayers have spoken, says the Father, and they have prognosticated the portents of destruction and darkness over the earth. Yet have I not said in My Word that the fool answers a matter before he hears it? They only have part of the picture, and they have not taken My Cross into account. And, yes, I spoke through the prophet Joel that there would be a day of the outpouring of My Spirit—that it would be a day of darkness and gloom.

But the darkness and gloom is for the enemies of My children. For I, likewise, said in the same breath by Joel that it would be as "morning spread on the mountains." There is a glory coming, says the Father, a light and an effulgence of majesty on the ramparts of the earth--not natural mountains, says the Father, but the mountains of majesty and the mountains of influence that I have revealed through My prophets in the present day.

I will adorn the mountains of influence with My majesty, says the Father, even in this day of turbulence and shaking. I am shaking all things so that My Kingdom and My Kingdom men and women will be the only ones left standing--not to conquer or condemn but to build and to love and extend life to the lifeless and love to the lovelorn.

Will you be My Kingdom man, says the Father? Will you be My Kingdom woman, says the Father? Will you boldly declare "My Kingdom come?" Let My boldness come upon you this day and be in your mouth and in your hands and in your hearts for you are the receptacles of My life, light, and glory. You are Mine, and I am yours, and we are going to take the prey and loose the captives, says the Father.

April 4th

The Father says, I am initiating transition in your life today. Change is not harmful. Change is beneficial. Change is the means by which I shape and mold you into My changeless image. The treasures of yesterday are the cast offs of today. If you cling to them, you become a castaway.

If you refuse to move on, you find yourself on the ash heap of life. And even from there, the Father says, I will give you beauty for ashes, but the ash-heap journey is an unnecessary trip if you listen to Me now and make the move.

April 5th

The Father says, there is a breach in your wall, and you have felt the intrusion. But, I am bringing God-speed acceleration to solve the problem. I will not be late although there have been times in the past you wondered where I was in the situation. Let not such thoughts enter into your mind because abandonment is not in My plan for you. I place no premium on your suffering, says the Father.

Why would I accept a condition in your life that I sent My Son to deliver you from? You have heard that teaching, and it did not sit right with you the first time. I am a God of blessings and abundance. I cannot give you what I do not have. There is no sickness in heaven, there is no poverty in the Glory, and there is no death in heaven. The only repository I provision you from is My riches in glory. When My hand reaches out to bless you, I do not draw from the inventories of hell. I provision you from the glories around My throne. Look for My "throne blessing" today. Expect it in the "now," says the Father, for it is the "now" I am positioning you to receive.

April 6th

The Father says, I bestow upon you today My unconditional love. I love you because I love you. I am foolishly fond of you. You can be yourself today because I love you. There is nothing that can make Me stop loving you. Love is not what I do. Love is who I am. Loving you today is as easy as being Myself. And since I will be Myself with you today, I give you permission to be yourself, to be who you are, and to be real with Me today. I did not send My Son to die in order to enable you to be other than who you are today. Those around you who claim to represent Me only do so honorably when they inspire you to unconsciously be yourself. After all, I created who you are, says the Father.

Why would I desire for you to put on airs or assume an affectation of someone other than who you are now? Change? Yes, all things change or die. When you see who I am, you will become like Me-- it is an inexorable law of transformation. Yet, how can you see Me unless you know My unconditional love? Raise your head today, child. Accept My love. Accept who I am, and you shall be free to accept who you are as well. The rest is just details.

April 7th

Dependence on Me is not a thing to be shunned. I am your breath. I am your life. By Me all things cohere and have their moment-by-moment existence. With one moment of inattention from Me, all the world would blink out of existence. You are as the pupil of My eye.

He who offends you offends the object of My affection. Keep your gaze on Me today. Turn your attention away from the prattling cries of the uninformed, who have no peace. I am your peace today. I am your joy. I bequeath you this day all that the Cross affords and call you to celebrate and rejoice in what I have bestowed.

April 8th

It is a new day, says the Father. Cast your eye upon the vistas of your future. Rejoice and be jubilant in what lies ahead. The future is not that which I would have you fear. I control the unknown parts of your life.

I am coming around the corner, and when you see what lies ahead, you will see Me looking back at you with laughter. Yes, you have made some mistakes. Yes, you have done things wrong and acted stupidly at times. But you cannot mess anything up that I cannot fix. I am the God of restoration and repair. I am the God that gives beauty and substance from ashes and desolation. Cast in your lot with Me today, and be merry in your day for this is the new day, says the Father, and you will never be the same!

April 9th

It is My glory to conceal. It is your glory to seek out. I created you to be inquisitive, says the Father. Your questions do not displease Me. Seek My face. Ask your questions for there is treasure in the learning that will only come to you if you ask.

I will awaken you in the night. I will startle you in the daytime. You will rejoice in the learning, and I will exalt in the teaching. I am the teacher. Let My doctrine distill in your spirit like the morning dew. That is My refreshing for you this day, and that is My rest that I impart to you even now.

April 10th

Spiritual deafness is a horrid thing, says the Father, for My voice is the delivery mechanism of My Kingdom. How can My Kingdom come upon one who will not hear? "He that has ears, let him hear." The choice is yours, says the Father. In the hearing of My voice comes righteousness, peace, and joy.

Let no one rob you of this joy by clapping their hands over your ears and saying, "Don't listen!" It is your Father who speaks and not another. It is your Maker who speaks the restorative word that brings the miracle to pass in your life. But, you must be willing to hear that which others have sought to withhold from you. You must be prepared to come into My presence and hear My voice undiluted by the thoughts of men. Therein lies your healing and liberty.

April 11th

The Father says today that you have been crying out for change. You have been seeking relief. I need some cooperation from you, however, to bring about the liberty and the transition you have requested. When the children of Israel sojourned in the wilderness, there came those times when they were called upon to break camp. There were some things they left behind and some things they took with them. The Father says, look at your life and simplify so you can fly.

It is time to jettison some things that have not served the interests of the Kingdom in your life, says the Father. No, there is no need to stand on ceremony or long, tearful soul-searching. Just stand up and walk out! Walk out of the bondages of habit, hardship, and heartbreak. Loose yourself from the bonds of illegitimate authority. Cast yourself into the billows of My purposes, says the Father, and I will be there to sustain and maintain your every move.

April 12th

The Father says today, I did not call you to enshrine the bones of unbelief that have bleached in the wilderness. The hour is come to break the ossuaries (the bone boxes of dead religion) and cross over the barriers of faith bearing the ark of My presence on your shoulders. Rise up! Advance toward the horizons of impossibility. Yes, they have said it could not be done, but who are they anyway? My voice is the voice of challenge and the voice of change.

As you walk into your own home under the lintel of the entrance, take possession of what I have given you. Demand the enemy to make his exit from your life and from your loved ones! It is time for an eviction, says the Father. It is time to evict poverty, evict lack, and evict sickness, sorrow, and brokenness of heart! Even this day--right now--I am putting "throne authority" behind your words and commissioning you to verbalize on earth what I am promising to do from the heavens on your behalf, says your Father.

April 13th

The Father says, Up! Up! Look up for I am sending a download from heaven! I am provisioning you with My wisdom for the situations of life that are before you. I have patterned for you an exit strategy. Now, walk out! Leave behind the barrier-bound, small-minded naysayers, and walk into My eternal "yes and amen!" Do not fall into the error of saying that you will wait for an opportune time.

I am the God of time, and I am the God of your now. Step forward and step out! Put your foot in the neck of your enemies, and declare the victory that unconditional love affords you this day, says the Father. Trust Me for the acceptable outcome, and trust Me for the deliverance you have been crying out to overcome. Even today I am visiting you with salvation, rest, and the approbation of your Father which is in heaven.

April 14th

The Father says today that your hope lies in your trust in Me and not any earthly thing. The economy is not your hope. The political process is not your hope. The leaders of nations are not your hope. I am your hope and I change not. I am the same yesterday, today and forever and I will never leave you and never forsake you.

Listen to My voice and not the voices of those who cannot look past the false security of human vanity. They are crying "Calamity, Calamity!" They are looking for a savior and have forsaken the Rock of their Salvation! I laid the foundation says the Father and they have forsaken the foundation that I have laid. But for those who trust in My name and yield to My voice I will yet suckle you at the bosom of My bounty and My provision.

Take heed to My voice and quiet yourself within your heart. Though the blind rage against the blind you are not blind for I will cause you to see My kingdom that you may participate with what I am doing and saying in your life. Fear not and be not disheartened. Though men's hearts fail them for fear and their courage flee away like a frightened animal, I will be your courage and will cause you even in the midst of the chaos of life to ride on the high places of the earth.

April 15th

The Father says today that the race is not for the swift nor the battle to the strong. I am the deciding factor in the conflict you are facing at this time. There is no strategy and no tactic that will assure victory. I am the way—I am your way. I will see you through. Look not to the right or to the left. Look not to the arm of flesh or to the natural resources available to you for your answers.

In the Prophet Isaiah's day, the nation of Israel looked to Egypt to be their ally and failed. See that Emmanuel on the inside of you is the "all sufficient one." I am of sufficient strength to preserve, protect, and provision you. This is My gift. This is the gift of Myself prearranged 2000 years ago for this hour and this time in your life. Lean on Me. Lean into Me for I am leaning into you right now.

April 16th

The thing you are facing right now is not about you being tempted, says the Father. It is about My faithfulness. It is true that your present distress did not take Me by surprise. I am not the orchestrator of the pressures of life for I place no premium upon your suffering or pain. Focus on My faithfulness. Do not look at the turbulence around you as though it would swallow you up. Keep your gaze fixed upon Me and Me alone. Never in the history of mankind has there ever been one event, one moment, one situation that the Cross did not provide for and make a way of escape.

Escape to My presence this day, says the Father. Yes, they want your every waking thought to be about them. They are demanding,

"What are you going to do?" Here is what you are going to do. You are going to be an imitator of Me. You are going to do what I would do if I was facing your circumstance because I am facing your circumstance. I am in you. I am bunkered inside of you, and you are bunkered inside of Me. We are going to get through this together and look back in laughter at the adventure and blessings that unfolded just when you thought all was lost.

April 17th

How do you like the day I made for you today? Earth and sky, day and night, are all tailor-made for your well-being and blessing. For a time the enemy is the "god" of this world, but I am the God of the heavens and the earth. I have scribed My goodness and My faithfulness upon the heavens. The very DNA, the double-helix structures in your DNA, is singing of My greatness and My watchfulness over you. It is a song of love and a song of passion. Those who claim to represent Me have gotten Me all wrong--I am a God of passion.

I do not casually look on while you are wondering where I am in your circumstance. Since the blood of the Cross fell to earth, I cannot take My eyes off of you. My Son paid the price that I might look nakedly upon you with all your failings and yet find ground to bless and encourage you. Yes, there are things in your life that do not make Me smile. But the blood negates your failures and transmits My forgiveness to you. You must forgive yourself. You must stop listening to those who do not forgive you. In the end of the matter, says the Father, the only opinion that matters is Mine for My thoughts are eternal and unchanging. The thoughts of men are fleeting, chaotic, and vain even when they try to focus on Me. They allow themselves to be distracted by thoughts that did not originate in My grace. So, set your heart on Me today for I have set My heart upon you.

April 18th

Can you imagine the world I have planned for you? In your mind can you conceive the soaring happiness I have inventoried for you in the heavens? I have signed the work order and dispatched the shipment. The angels are bringing onto you now the package I have prepared for you before the world began. It is My kairos destiny for this hour in your life. When I placed you in the earth, says the Father, I was not cavalier or curious about what would happen. I did not sit back then and say, "Watch this!" No, I have hovered and fluttered about you every second and every moment to superintend and provide much needed assistance.

You are that which thrills Me, says the Father. You are the reason I "get out of bed" every morning. If I had a bed and took sleep, I would lay awake at night thinking about you and what I would do to bless you next. Adjust your thinking to My love, care, and passion for you. Jettison every picture or image of Me that distorts the intense love that I have for you and am showing you every moment. The only time I have to share My love with you is now, says the Father, for I do not live in the past or the future. I am a God of the "now," and now is when I desire to pour out my "now" upon your life. Open your now to Me, says the Father! Open your now to me as a vessel opened and presented to me that I might fill it with My goodness. Even this day I will cause you to overflow with My provisioning grace if you will accept it as so and say, "Yes, Father! Do what you said!"

April 19th

I am a consuming fire, says the Father. It is not just what I do; it is who I am. Those things in your life that do not originate in Me or reflect My nature are consumed by My presence. When you allow yourself to be attached to those things that do not reflect My character, you will then feel the heat. You can even be damaged if you refuse to relinquish that which the fire of Myself is consuming. So, let go, says the Father, because I did not create you to be combustible.

I created you to walk around in the eternal now with Me. Grieve not for the things that consume away. Yes, they will melt with heat-- even fervent heat. That burning is preferable to the decay those things, those relationships, those habits of life would bring into your heart. Just go ahead and let go! Laugh! If you then have regret, says the Father, let My love be your consolation. I will mollify your wounds with the ointments of My presence, and you will be healed and changed and refreshed even this day.

April 20th

The Father says, I have set you in your life even as I set Adam in the garden. I have infused you with a charge and an authority to tend and to keep it. I will superintend your blessings by the administration of your words. Open your mouth very wide, and I will be that which fills it. Inventory your surroundings. Take stock of your circumstances. Address the issues that are before you with the verbalizations of faith. The decrees that you establish will be the parameters that will contain My glory and the riches therein that are released to you through your faith-filled prayers.

My effluence will dispel the darkness of lack, sickness, heartbreak, and desperation. I will engulf your life as you declare "My Kingdom come" in your garden, says the Father. Your deliverance is waiting for the occasion of your faith-filled prayers and declarations. Yes, I will work, but I will only work with you for you are My sons and My daughters. You are royalty to Me, and I would that you wield the scepter of dominion over your earth and over your life and the lives of others. They are looking for someone to speak to the storm and say, "Be still!" No longer allow your lips to be silent. If you say it, I will do it. If you are silent, I thereby await your words. Upon your words the blessings and graces of deliverance will rise up before you. There are no pennies from heaven, says the Father. There is only the "gold of God" that manifests at the behest of your words, which I am calling forth even today, My son and My daughter.

April 21st

I am the Lord your God. Do you really think that situation is too hard for Me? I am not like those who claim to have faith but blind their eyes to the "hard" cases, the wheelchair bound, the blind, or the infirm. There are no gradients of power in the strength of My arm when I act, says the Father. I speak and the seas boil and the earth is moved off of its axis. I glance and the forests tremble at the might of My eyelids. You are the pupil of My eye. I am not reluctant to move in your life. I gain no pleasure or achieve no purpose in seeing you go without to suffer or to labor in bonds and bondage.

Rise up! Shake yourself for I am reordering things in your life. I will no longer allow you to live without joy. There are those who have defined service to Me as a limpid, bleak, joyless existence. They have Me all wrong! I sit in the heavens and laugh, and at My laughter the thunder rolls and the lightning flashes. I come down on behalf of My children, who cry out to me. So, be silent no longer. Open your mouth and cry out. Return your cries to Me. Call forth My faithfulness, and I will do it. Will I not change the unchangeable, subvert the unacceptable, restore the unredeemable, raise up the irretrievable, and make your night of darkness as the noonday of blessing even this day, says the Father?

April 22nd

The Father says, I am calling you to rest in Me today. My Holy Spirit is in abeyance where the will of man is exerting itself. When you try to take over the circumstance, look over your shoulder. You will see Me standing there with arms folded. My Spirit is in the ascendancy when you calm yourself in the midst of the frenzy of life and wait on My salvation. Others may scurry about, wringing their hands and crying, but I put in your mouth the laugh of faith.

Let the belly laugh of joy burst forth out of your mouth. They will say you are inappropriate. They will say you have lost your mind. They will say you do not understand the gravity of the situation. But you will answer them (who are they anyway) and say, "No you don't understand the gravity of my God!" For your God, child, is the weighty one, and I am about to bring the weight of My strength and what I can do into your life, and nothing will ever be the same again. You will look back and smile, realizing that the storm of life that you thought was the end of all things is now just a footnote of a season of time and a sweet testimony of how I came through for you at the appointed hour.

April 23rd

You are My transmitter, says the Father. All My goodness, all My grace, and all My power is poised for emission into your life and circumstance. My hand hovers over the release, waiting for the occasion of your prayers of petition. I would that you open your mouth wide and say, "Father . . . thy Kingdom come into this life you have given me . . . ." Be specific. Be bold. Ask largely for you are the transmitter of My glory.

You are the conduit of heaven to earth. You are the spillway of the glory over the brim of the heavens into the deepest crevices of your life. I am ready to pour out, says the Father. I simply wait for the occasion of your audacious prayers.

April 24th

The Father says, you have cried out to Me for acceleration, but turbulence comes with acceleration. There are no timetables engraved in stone. Time and happenstance are on the negotiating table when you and I go about My business together. Some things you thought would happen sooner will happen later. Some things you thought would happen later will happen sooner.

My priority is not seeing that certain things happen at certain times; rather, my priority is that you survive the process. So, I say again that with acceleration comes turbulence. You will transition through the turbulence if you lay hold of Me and cling to Me. My arms will encompass you, and I will hold you to My bosom. You know exactly why you received this word today.

April 25th

No greater love than this: that a man lay down his life for his friend. I laid down My life, and I took it again. And, in taking it up I took you with it. I led captivity captive. When I took up My life and exited the tomb, your life, your soul, and your consciousness were attached to My life by divine sovereignty. No man, no demon, nor any outside force controls your life, says the Father. You belong to Me.

I will assert My claim on your life at the opportune time, and you will be freed from the illegitimate authority that has laughably asserted its jurisdiction on your affairs. I will sweep them aside like yesterday's leavings, says the Father. Put your trust in Me. Look to the dawn of My deliverance. Let the laugh of faith be on your lips and in your mouth. They do not know who they angered when they touched the apple of My eye.

April 26th

I have given every creature natural defenses, says the Father. I have given you the power of articulate speech. There is a defense I have given you that cannot be overthrown. It is the ability to frame a little word called "NO!" There are those placing demands on your time and resources that are demanding a yes from you today. You have My permission to turn them away. In fact, you have My encouragement to do so. Have I not said your life is not your own? If your life is not your own, how much more so is it not theirs to dispose of at their whim?

They will say you are unwise and that you did not think it through. They may scoff and say, "We thought you loved us." They may say, "And you call yourself a Christian!" Just laugh, says the Father, knowing that I told you how they would react. Those weak protestations are simply the last gasp of illegitimate authority.
What are you going to do with all that time on your hands now that they do not have you running about serving their every whim? You are going to do what you see the Father do, and in so doing I will enter into your day and bring My blessing and My purpose to bear in your life and the lives of many.

April 27th

I am the God that brought manna from heaven and water from rock, says the Father. I can bring gas from a pump, peace from a war, and provision from a downward-spiraling economy. I will be known as the provisioner of the faithful. Put your attention on Me. Be drawn to My purpose and fulfill My mandate as I daily reveal to you the steps you are to take.

This day I set a difference between the children of light and the children of men, says the Father. Men may wring their hands and show their frustration, anger, and fear. But looking around they shall see My sons and My daughters composed, confident, and worry-free. You are

My sons, and you are My daughters. Look for the water from the rock and manna from the heavens. Expect atypical, unusual, unique events of supply and support to come to you even today, says the Father. Let your quietness and confidence in the storm become the beacon of strength that the sons of men are crying out for in this hour.

April 28th

The Father says, make My presence your priority today. Yes, there are many demands on your time and attention, yet even today I would deliver you from the tyranny of the "urgent." There is but one thing that is important, says the Father, and that is to sit at My feet. Gather yourself to My footstool. Turn your countenance upward toward Me, and set your affections fully on Me.

Allow Me to kiss your face and wrap My arms around you. Experience the bosom of My embrace this day. The frenzied activities of the world will swirl around you as the currents of a raging flood, but you will be safe and insulated in the folds of My good comfort.

April 29th

The Father says today, if you seek My face, you will see My hand. If you seek My judgment, you will receive My mercy. There is a rejoicing that mercy has prepared over judgment in your life. The table is spread, and the angels assigned to your portion have arrayed themselves in celebratory garb. The King has come to make His appearance for you have been included in the festivities of His favor today, says the Father. Yes, it is true that your detractors have cried before Me day and night because you have not lived up to their expectations. However, I do not hear their protestations, and I do not hear their accusations.

The blood that My Son shed for you has deafened me to the rage of your accusers. Relax, says the Father! What would you say that I should do unto you this day? Ask largely. Ask expansively. Let your asking reflect the breadth of your confidence in your Father for I will not fail you. The only prayer I will not answer is that prayer which proceeds from a small faith in a distant god. That is not who I am in your life. I am as close as the breath of your nostrils. Your inhalation is My exhalation. Your exhalation is My inhalation. In you I choose to live and breathe and have My being. I invite you to live and breathe and have your being in Me today.

April 30th

The Father says today that the results are in and the tally is now completed. Those that are for you are more and greater than those that are against you. There is no obstacle in your path that will not yield to My words in your mouth, says the Father. No barrier can withstand the onslaught of angelic dominion that attends the articulate release of your faith-filled words. The lies of the enemy have spelled out an end and a termination.

That is not, however, what I have said about you, is it? You are not what they say you are this day. You will not see the outcome they have portended in their hate and unbelief. What was the last thing I told you? Trust Me for the outcome. Let your words and your actions reflect the confidence you have in Me in the face of the flagrant attempts of the enemy and circumstance to put the lie to My promise. Your heart is the seat of My authority in your life. I have chosen to put My name there, and it is there in your heart I will take My rest. It is there that I will laugh at My enemies and mock at their pitiful attempts to contradict the blessing that I have surely promised you even in this hour, says your Father. Look for it even today.

May 1st

There is a serpent in your garden, says the Father. Say within your heart, "I will not be fooled again." I have armed you, and I have equipped you. Open the eyes of your spirit and see that the ax I equipped John the Baptist with I have put in your hand. Lay the ax at the root of the tree where the serpent is taking his refuge. Let the boughs of the tree of the knowledge of good and evil be hewn down in your life, says the Father.

Say within your heart, "I will only partake of the tree of life from this day forward." I am calling you beyond your intellect and beyond your current understanding of My ways, says the Father. I am placing a demand upon your ability to act out of your intuitive mind in order that you might follow Me wherever I may lead and even if I choose to take you where your natural mind goes "tilt" and makes no sense.

You might look to the right or to the left, says the Father. I understand that, but you dare not look back for that would make you unfit for the Kingdom that is coming upon you even today. Say within your heart, "I will follow the impetus of the Kingdom of my Father today, and I will only respond to His voice." In so doing, says the Father, you purchase for yourself an adoption and an authority that will cause you to become a whole other class of believer. As you follow Me through the hard lessons, I will bring you to a place in Me that everything you say or do will become as effective as if I said it or did it myself. Yea, I will not allow one of your words to fall to the ground, says the Father. Get out your garden hoe, and deal with that pathetic little serpent in your garden. If you will just do this, we have great days ahead of us.

May 2nd

I am seated within your heart, says the Father, and I have seated you on My throne. Regardless of how you feel or what you think, I have seated you high above all principality, power, problems, or predicaments. You are in Christ, and My Son is at My right hand. Can you hear My voice as I whisper in your ear, "You are more than a conqueror?" Let the laugh of faith melt all your enemies and problems and predicaments like wax in the flame. They are no match for who I am in you and who you are in Me. Rejoice in the contest, says the Father.

When the pressure is on and the contest is hot, look in the mirror and smile saying, "It makes me feel so alive!" For greater is the pressure on the inside of My Kingdom flowing out of you than the pitiful pressures of life that laughably presume to paint some doom-and-gloom picture over your head. Open your mouth and say, "Bah, ha, ha!" Watch your enemies scatter before you--enemies of poverty, lack, sickness, doubt, and depression. Watch them all flee before you because I am standing behind you daring them to give you one moment's resistance. They see the fire in My eye, and they run far and fast to escape My wrath. I will no longer tolerate the spirits of despondency to weigh you down. I am lightening your load, says the Father. Rejoice, for the days ahead are days of glory as you pursue your purpose in Me.

May 3rd

The Father says today, "Stand and deliver the decrees of your God!" Do not fear to measure the depth of the problem or the scope of the challenges that are facing you even now. The fact that your problem can be measured is because it has an end. My supply is boundless. It cannot be tapped or drained, says the Father. I am breathing upon the empty places in your heart and in your life. I am breathing on your health, your relationships, and your finances for I will have you unencumbered in My service, says the Father. I say again, let your mouth deliver and decree in articulate speech the decree and petition that I have placed in your heart.

My breath is provisioning and changing in your life. Speak to your health, speak to your body, and speak to your relationships, vocation, and finances. Command them to become vibrant and robust with the life that I am breathing into you even now. It is the hour of change. You have cried out to Me for change. You have requested, cajoled, begged, asked, knocked, and sought, and I have not been sleeping or ignoring you. If you listen, you will feel the rumble under your feet as I am coming swiftly to open the door of blessing and opportunity. Look for the opening you have been praying for even today, and when you see it (even slightly), launch into it with all your being for I am with you and will prosper you in your way.

May 4th

The Father says, I have put long life, length of days, and peace aside in My glory as a stipend for you to draw upon as needed. There is no foreshortening in My plan. There is no deficit that serves My purpose. I set no premium upon suffering, lack, or want in your life. To withdraw from you in these matters would be to alter My nature for I am Jehovah-Jireh, your provisioner. I am the unchanging, unalterable, constant Father who brought you to birth for this time and this hour.

From time immemorial (before the foundation of the earth was laid) I carried in My hands the spark of life that was released into the earth with your soul attached at the moment of conception. You were with Me and in Me in the eternities, joyous and beholding My order and purpose for your life. That purpose is being threaded out on the weaver's beam of time on a day-by-day basis, and it is a tapestry of blessing and grace and forgiveness in the miraculous. Throughout all the golden thread, My watchful, loving, and passionate care is present. Trust in Me for every care today. Trust in Me for the dream for you did not arrive at your dreams by yourself. You and I dreamed them together in the eternities and launched you to their fulfillment when you were born into the earth. There is no disappointment in Me, says your Father.

May 5th

My Kingdom cannot be domesticated, says the Father. My Kingdom is in you. The portion of Myself that resides in your being will not be contained. My will for your life is not about containment but about activation and launching. Who I am in you is rising up even today, says the Father. I am breaking down the barriers and taking no prisoners.

The enemy of your soul will capitulate! Speak My mind against the enemy's works in your life this day. Bring My words against the bulwarks of lack, doubt, heartbreak, loss, and unbelief. I will not be bound by time, circumstance, predicament, or problems, and neither will I have you bound. Yes, the breaker anointing is upon you, but it must break over you before it can set others free as well. Receive the breaker anointing, says the Father. Let it become verbally articulate in your mouth, and watch the outcome that will begin to emerge before the sun sets this day.

May 6th

My blood is speaking, says the Father. The peal of its cry broke forth on Calvary, and it reverberated down through the centuries and is thundering over you now. It is declaring, "Thou art clean!" It is declaring you are whole. It is declaring your chains are broken, your purse is mended, and no longer will the lack, death, defeat, and sorrows of the past define your future. Abel's blood cried out for vengeance on his brother, but the blood of the Son sounds forth a higher testimony.

When My Son entered the holiest of holies in the heavens, He cleansed the way between you and Me with His freshly spilled blood. As your high priest, He sprinkled His own blood upon the altar upon which your prayers would be offered. That blood sanctifies the altar of your petitions. Neither your failings, your past, nor your shortcomings or even your sins can pollute the altar that the blood of the Son has cleansed! Let your heart pursue after Me, says the Father. Let your heart pursue hot after Me for I will be found of those who pursue Me along the blood-cleansed way that is the person of My Son, who sits at the right hand ever interceding for you. You are forgiven! You are cleansed! I declare your deliverance this day, says your God and your Maker and your Father.

May 7th

Perplexity of spirit is not the natural state of a child of God, says the Father, and it is not an environment where I will leave you. Even when you do damage to yourself through ignorance, fear, or sin, no weapon formed against you will prosper. Does your heart condemn you? Bah, ha, ha, says the Father. I am greater than your heart, and it is the I am on the inside of you rumbling His thunder against the enemies of your soul!

Even this day I will release My Spirit upon you. Expect the unusual, unique, and unexpected eventualities of the Kingdom to seek you out on angel's wings and find you even in the deepest calamities. Even from the deepest hell, I will draw you and redeem you with the purchase price of My Son. Fret not, says the Father. Neither let your heart be overburdened with care for I am sending necessary assistance and needed superintendence over your life today. Do not be afraid. Do not be tremulous. Be confident in your God, and let your praises ring out even in the teeth of your enemy, says the Father.

May 8th

The Father says today that your worship is about more than emotional release or spiritual catharsis. Worship that is heart-felt and verbally articulate deposits the incense of your prayers on the altar in the heavens. The coals of this incense become a sweet aroma before My throne that fuels the return of that worship to the earth in the form of answered prayers. In the beginning the line of Cain was the first to experiment with music. They understood the power of melody and praise, so they built a tower to appropriate by dark arts the resources laid in store by My hand in the glories. I confounded them and ended their strategy.

There is a dearth in the land of answered prayer, says the Father. There have been leanness and resource shortfalls. I am correcting them by the power of My hand. This is the day I am answering prayers on a 24-hour cycle. Bring your requests to Me today. Ask me for the bread that provisions you for this day; tomorrow will accord itself its own challenges. Let your prayers be moistened with the oil of My Spirit and offered in the melodic strains of praise, worship, and adoration. The angels assigned to your life are awaiting the kindling of answers on that designated place on the altar where your name is engraved. Offer up your incense day by day, says the Father. Do not allow the sleep to depart from your eyes before you ascend in worship that you might descend in warfare. I will war with you and give you victory over all your enemies.

May 9th

I am bringing a shift in your life beginning today, says the Father. We are moving away from the dry spell into a season of moistening and rain. Your lands have been dry and cracked with no growth and no provender, but that is about to change in a big way. No longer will you wonder when the blade, the ear, and the full corn in the ear will appear.

This is the hour that the ploughman will overtake the reaper. This is the hour and the day that you will taste and know me as the God who is more than enough. Empty your stores, says the Father, and dispense your surplus to the poor in the streets for I am sending fresh inventories from the Glory to stock your life with every good thing. Are you ready? Reach out by faith and by declarations that are verbally articulate and expansive beyond all reckoning. Ask not a small thing for I am not a small God. Ask expansively of that which you would that I do unto you, and you will see it break ground even today.

May 10th

New growth, says the Father, is the end result of faithful planting. This day's harvest was determined by yesterday's planting. I will be faithful to send the manna when needed, but I have called you to be a farmer in the things of the Spirit. Seed your words of faith into the earth. Plant your words of faith according to the crops of blessing that you have needed and that you desire.

I will rain down upon those plantings, add My Spirit to the soil of your life, and cause a harvest (even a bountiful harvest) to come forth at the appointed time. It is my purpose to work with you and not simply for you, says the Father. Come along beside Me as we sculpt the landscape of your future for I will do nothing without your cooperation and consent. As you consent to My will and My plans, you will find the emergence of harvest and blessing beyond your expectations for I am the "more-than-enough" God.

May 11th

I am searching you out in the night seasons, says the Father. The scrutiny of My eye is examining every fiber of your being. There is nothing hidden from the intensity of My divine inquiry of your innermost being. Do you know what I have found? I have found nothing that dampens My love for you. I have found nothing that disqualifies you from your Kairos destiny. I have found no reason to altar My plan or change My direction of blessing and abundance that has been accorded to you from the glories.

I will be speaking to you in dreams for the next few nights, says the Father. Hearken to My voice for I am dislodging the inert opinions in your spirit that only serve to distract from My great purpose in your life. I am sealing My instruction within your inner man, and I am preparing you for a greater dominion in the garden of your life. Reach out to Me. Look for Me in the common places. I will be found of you, and I will join Myself to you in a fresh reclamation project of blessing this day.

May 12th

The human spirit is the hearth of My creative power. I have set eternity in your heart, and I have set temporal dominion in your spirit that you might rule and reign with Me now. What things would you have Me do for you, says the Father? What changes would you have Me enact and what deliverances would you desire that I bring to manifestation in your life and the lives of your loved ones?

Do you understand that I will not let one word from your mouth fall to the ground? A careless word is a dangerous thing, says the Father. Careless words render the words of My power inert in your heart. So, let your mouth pray and your opinions remain silent. Out of the ashes of disappointment and unanswered petitions will arise a glory and a habitation that will give you rest and launch you into your prophetic destiny. Stand forth and obey the impetus of My Spirit, urging you even at this hour. The blessing of My hand is "on-hand" ready to be deployed on your behalf.

May 13th

You are getting in deep, says the Father. You are getting deeper into Me. You are getting further from the shores of religious convention. Go ahead and dive off the deep end in Me! You are ranging farther afield from the restrictions of mortality into My limitless grace. This is where the miracles begin to happen.

You asked to come here. Did you think there was any capacity in My Kingdom that I would deny you? Go ahead and vault over the rail. You know you want to take a walk on the waves with Me. I am as excited as you are, says the Father. Is it not about time? You know exactly why you received this today.

May 14th

I invented exhilaration, says the Father. I did not create the earth in a dispassionate or aloof frame of mind--I shouted! I thundered!

I bellowed, and the waves crashed, and the dry land appeared! My dancing hand leaped and spun across the universe as I was in the act of creating that which I intended for your joy. Be exhilarated in Me, says your Father. Go ahead and do exploits--be bold!

Charge the trenches of the enemy of your soul. He thinks he can keep you from your blessings. He thinks that he can hold your loved ones captive and keep you suppressed and impoverished. He has no clue who I am in you. Go ahead and let fly your passion, your great heart, and your hopes and dreams, says the Father. I spun them on the tapestry of your days before you were ever born. Today is your day if you "just will"!

May 15th

If you pause in your spirit just a moment, says the Father, you can hear it. Can you hear it? TICK! TICK! TICK! It is the "joy bomb" about to explode in your life. I am bringing a shift because I cannot allow you to live without joy any longer. I am extracting you from the fellowship of the "joy-less." It is true that they think they excluded you, but it was My idea, says the Father. Do not let them get to you. I am bringing you out so I can bring you into the joy--the dancing, spinning, shouting, dizzying joy that is My Kingdom! As you spin and dance and shout, the prison doors are opening, and the miracles are beginning to coalesce on all the surfaces of your life.

Look for oil. Look for gold. Look for odd, strange, and even silly manifestations. I love to confound those that think they have Me all figured out. Today is the day I change everything, says the Father. Go ahead and step into it. Get it all over you and roll around in it. Get messy, uncouth, and be an embarrassment to your religious friends because they are next. The joy you feel and that I am making available is about to pour over them. What is all over you today is going to get all over them!

May 16th

I will never leave you. I will never forsake you. I will never stop loving you because I will never stop being love. Love is who I am. Yes, there are those who have misrepresented Me. There are those in your life (even in the last 24 hours) that underscored for you just how lethal dead religion is and how barren and bankrupt it is as well. Take heart, says the Father. For Me there is no turning back now.

The cross of My Son was a "no going back, point-of-no return" outpouring of love from My heart for you. The Cross was eternity's tipping point. I will not be turned back, and I will not be dissuaded in My "hot pursuit" of My love and passion for you, says the Father. Just slow down a moment. Just hesitate a moment in My peace. I will bowl you over and bundle you up in an embrace that will leave nothing left but My love for you. Receive My love, says the Father. Come away My beloved!

May 17th

You are better off outside the camp and better off in the company of My misfits than with the most respectable impediments to My Kingdom purposes. In the company of the worldly-wise, foolishness is a virtue. Have they called you names? Have they maligned your integrity? Have they questioned your motives? Welcome to the inner circle, says the Father.

Leave your cross and nails with the coat-check girl, and come into a closed session with My misbegotten, misunderstood, misquoted, misfits, and mighty men. I can use you now. You are shed of the good opinion of men, and I can now clothe you with Myself. The opinions of men are fleeting and fickle, but My glory is eternal. It is that glory I clothe you with now.

May 18th

The enemy of your soul is in an all-out effort to stratify your life with disappointment and loss. His purpose is to exploit and mine veins of bitterness from the sediments and bedrock of your mind, memory, and emotions. He thinks he has hit the "mother-lode." I am about to show him to the door. My joy, My Kingdom, and My indwelling Spirit are the antidotes to reversing the waves of bitterness and sorrow that besiege your life from time to time. I am your exit strategy, says the Father. Take your refuge in Me while I heal your earth.

Out of the ashes of past hurts and sorrows, I am crafting a testimony of grace, faithfulness, and healing. I will not allow the enemy to be the architect of your life, says the Father. In the days ahead I will be requisitioning your cooperation in a kingdom reclamation project. I will begin in your past and will be encompassing your present and reaching far into your future with My promises, My purposes, and My pursuits. I will leave nothing out. I will not neglect to spade under the entirety of your life in order that I might cause it to become a container of My great purpose.

When you hear the approaching rumble of My angelic earth-moving equipment, fear not. I am only coming to shake out every bondage, every pocket of grief and hurt, and pour in their place the foundations of My glory, honor, and virtue that will be the groundwork for the days ahead. I have a great work for you to do, and I will not have you distracted by the demonic squatters who think they have the right to camp on your life. I will drive them off and make your life a barracks of angelic hosts. You can expect to see them at work in your life in the coming days. Do not be surprised. They are not there to draw attention to themselves; they are there to execute the blueprint blessing in your life that the blood of Christ ratified 2000 years ago.

May 19th

I have made you of quick understanding, says the Father. I have put life-giving understanding on the inside of you. This is so you might know what to do when others run out of ideas. Merely human solutions fail to solve most problems. Man wants to cover up, compromise, and negotiate. However, I will be known in your midst by My name, Jehovah-nissi. I have raised in you the banner of My Kingdom. The enemy has howled his disapproval and turned all his fury on My purposes in your heart and life. Say within your heart, "I will mock when calamity cometh, for my God is more than enough!"

I am not negotiating with the enemy for your release from the bondages of the domain of darkness. There will be no armistice and no peace talks with the adversary. There will be one end and only one that I will accept, says the Father. Do you know what it is? It will be the end that leaves you with your foot in the neck of the enemy of your souls and the sword of the Lamb in your hand held high in victory. Fear not the onslaught of the enemy that is coming against you at this time. Open your mouth wide in the face of desolation, isolation, poverty, lack, and disease. Open your mouth and decree the decrees of one who is more than a conqueror for I am speedily hastening to your defense even this day, says the Father.

May 20th

Illegitimate authority shall not rule over you today or any future day, says the Father. Set yourself to abide in Me as I abide in you. Abide in the vine because I am in your life. By abiding in Me the spiritual predators and the religiously misinformed will be unable to contaminate My voice in your life. Say within your heart as you rise each morning, "I will only do what I see My Father do." And, in that simple transaction I will step into your mind and spirit to direct your day and cause you to walk in Kingdom privileges and prerogatives.

Abiding in Me and walking in Me is as simple as relinquishing your opinions and surrendering to the moment-by-moment drawing and directing of the indwelling of My Spirit. You have asked for this. You have longed for it. You have wondered what it would be like to live and move and have your being in Me. Today is your day. Step into Me today. Surrender your mind to Me even as you surrendered your heart so long ago. Breathe Me in and breathe Me out, and I will synchronize the streams of your merely-human thoughts to My divine thought. I will be there certifying every word, every action, and every turn as you learn afresh and anew what it is to cooperate and to flow with My Spirit. This is what My Kingdom is like on a moment-by-moment basis. This is the mystery and the adventure of allowing Me to be manifest in your "now" experience.

May 21st

The Father says today that you knew this day would come. This is the day everything changes. This is the day that you deposit your full confidence, trust, and reliance upon Me in the very area of your life that represents your greatest struggle. It is water-walking time! It is time to get your feet wet! I will not fail you, and I will not allow the boisterous circumstances (which threaten to swallow you up) shipwreck your life.

As you vault over the rail and make your way to Me, I want you to think about what you are moving toward and what you are leaving behind. You are leaving behind intimidation, hesitation, fear, and complacency. You are moving toward My open embrace. You are leaving behind the company of the religiously uninformed and joining the company of the embattled few who dared to nakedly believe in the audaciousness of My promises. I will not fail you, and I will not allow you to fail Me. This is that day--up to the rail now! Watch that first step as it is a big one. What a thrill! Come to Me. Join Me for a walk on the waters of adversity. You know you want to and you know exactly why you received this word on this particular day.

May 22nd

Allow Me to be common bread in your life today, says the Father. To merely place Me on reverent display in your life betrays the intention of the Cross. I would that you partake of Me, consume Me, allow Me to fill your belly with the warmth of who I am and what I can do in and through you. Are you naked? Then clothe yourself with My Spirit. Are you hungry? Then fill yourself with the sustenance that I am this day. Are you destitute? In need? Impoverished?

When no man cares for your lot, says the Father, I am there to be your provision. Do you believe this or have you accepted the lie that circumstance, experience, and the religiously uninformed have promulgated in your mind? Cry out to Me today. My hand awaits the receipt of your prayers that are verbal, articulate, and precise in any situation. I will do nothing but that you first ask Me. Even this day upon the asking, says the Father, I will melt the hills and part creation itself in My molten, white-hot haste to come down and show Myself faithful in matters both great and small that pertain to your well-being.

May 23rd

My Kingdom is not event-driven, says the Father. My Kingdom does not proceed according to a set of dates on a calendar. My Kingdom is not a chronological agenda. My Kingdom does not come with passive observation. My Kingdom, rather, is a present participation. My Kingdom advances as who you are in the world becomes eclipsed by who I am in you. Can you sense My presence expanding in you today? I am not only walking with you today, but I am walking in you.

As I blur the lines of who I am and who you are, I want you to experience the exhilaration of My love. Being one with you is the consummation of My love and My life on the inside of you. That love and that life is a life-giving, problem-ruling, decree-making force that will sweep across your life and reorder all your affairs, circumstances, and situations according to My promises. Yield to My Spirit, says the Father. Yield to the increase of My governing Holy Spirit down in the depths of your being. The changes you are crying out for and the meaning you are looking for in life are not found by scouring current events for a sign of outward things. That which you long for is abiding in the depths of your being where I make My throne over your life. Yield to that and know that I am God, not only in the earth but in your life as well.

May 24th

I have not called you to live by your wits, says the Father, nor have I called you to employ reason, rationale, or logic to solve the sticky situations you face today. Your mind is not that part of you designed to rule and reign. Your mind is simply a servant intended to respond to the dictates of your spirit as I breathe My mind into the very fiber of your being.

Can you hear its objections and protests even now? The mind is a steward that has been unfaithful to the rulership of your spirit, says the Father. It is time to replace the sense-ruled mind into its subordinate place and into My life-giving Spirit. In so doing you allow the artistry of My hand to access the full pallet of your being and, consequently, to paint your life in the full, radiant pigments of My great purposes, says the Father.

May 25th

All prayer is answered on a 24-hour cycle, says the Father. Did I not say, "Take no thought for the morrow?" Was I mistaken perhaps? Did I misspeak? No, my child, listen to My words to you this day that there is no prayer intended for two days, two weeks, or two years from now. Today is the day of My mighty hand, says the Father. Tomorrow is but a figment of reality that may not come about according to your expectations.

Focus your faith, your petitions, and your asking on this day. In this day you will see My Spirit at work and My angels deployed on your behalf to meet every challenge, every need, every circumstance, and every situation.

May 26th

Love activates deliverance, says the Father. Love is the governor of My power and My grace because love is who I am. I am the Spirit of the Lord, the One in control of all matters and affairs of your life. Never allow any situation, person, or circumstance to impede or pollute My love flowing in your life. In that moment when love is diminished in your heart, I am diminished in your life. Yet, as you release My love toward others, My presence is amplified in your situation. Did you understand what I just said?

You can bring Me on the scene of your troubles by choosing to love. Choosing to love hastens My arrival in your circumstance. You have been asking, "Where are you in all of this, Lord?" Here is your answer. I am waiting on the ramparts of the glories for the occasion of your love. The expression of your love (reflecting My grace toward others) will cause My delivering hand to explode in your life and bring every blessing, deliverance, and answer that you seek.

May 27th

You have questioned Me about the angelic, says the Father.

Angels are not as complicated as you might think. They have one mandate and that is to attend My presence. If you need assurance that angelic assistance is being deployed in your life today, then allow My presence to resonate in you from the very moment you open your eyes. When an angel turns his scrutiny upon you, says the Father, he looks for one thing and one thing only--My presence.

My presence is the passion that drives an angel's fury against the enemy of your soul. When I say to you, "Magnify the Lord," I am not asking for Myself, says the Father. I am actually instructing you how to do your part when it comes to answered prayer. As you worship Me and glorify Me with your songs, words, prayers, and deeds, My angels depart from the heavens laden with answered prayer and deliverance on your behalf. Praise Me, says the Father. Lift up your voice today, and let your mouth worship and praise Me in verbally articulate and melodic tones. In so doing you hasten the angelic deliverance that is needed to set that plaguing circumstance in your life aright.

May 28th

It is getting crowded around you, says the Father. The angels assigned to your security and success knew the assault would come, and provision has been made for your protection. The blood line has been drawn, and beyond its boundary the enemy of your soul does hiss and spit and slither. Pay him no mind and neither give ear to the tongues of those who have lent their minds to the dark one, says the Father. You know who they are as they speak wrath, fear, loathing, and judgment against you. Say within your heart, "No weapon formed against me will prosper." In this saying the angelic hosts around you bristle and beat their swords against their shields to taunt the enemy.

Say within your heart, "I am more than a conqueror through Christ." The angels around you (upon hearing this) respond to your decrees with war cries that pierce the ears of the enemy and cause them not to think clearly. The battle raging around you is already won, says the Father. The victory celebration waits for the occasion of the release of your faith-filled words.

May 29th

My Spirit is in the ascendancy when your will is in abeyance, says the Father. Quiet yourself this day. Quiet your soul like a suckling child, and you will hear the answers to the questions you have been asking. I will not shout over the raging voices in your thoughts. I am speaking, I am articulating, and I am making known to you the wisdom and the understanding for the problem areas of your life. You must silence the undisciplined thoughts of your mind. You have even wondered if those voices were demonic, says the Father. No, they are simply unruly children--ungoverned objections to My Word, My Spirit, and My voice. They comprise the totality of what is called "the carnal mind."

In order to hear what I have been saying, says the Father, simply turn within yourself and say, "hush." You will be amazed at how responsive your inner man can be to that simple command. Then, get ready! Get a pen and a notebook before you. In fact, carry them with you at all times because you will begin to hear, perceive, and receive the torrents of wisdom and understanding and teaching that I want to give you. You will find relief and respite from the sense of isolation and fear and receive what I have always been answering, speaking, and delivering to you.

A new day has come, says the Father, and a day of constant ongoing communion with Me that you have asked for is here. You will enjoy it as you hearken to My instructions today.

May 30th

You have asked Me what is your place, says the Father. Your place is a position. It is your place to be seated with Me far above principalities and powers of darkness that seek to rule the earth. When you see the portion I have accorded to you, says the Father, you will realize that you are, in fact, a principality in the earth. I have placed you in the location where you are to serve as My agent to unseat the rulers of darkness and usurp their control over your villages, towns, and cities.

Did you think you would have to wait for the "after-life" before you would begin to rule and reign?

May 31ˢᵗ

You have resented being blamed, says the Father. This is because you did not realize that when others blame you (when you were only obeying Me) that they actually make you "God" in the situation. When those around you accuse and point the finger, they unknowingly sell their birthright and give you the authority in the circumstance at issue. Therefore, bless them this day, says the Father. They will never change until they experience My goodness. I know there are those who have counseled you to call down wrath upon their heads; that counsel is not of My Spirit but another spirit, says the Father.

It is My goodness that leads men to change their minds. They will change their minds about you and change their minds about Me when they see My goodness that you are about to pray down into their lives. Bless, says the Father. Bless and do not curse. Sweet water and bitter water do not belong at the same fountain. When you curse, you only bring decay and misery to your own life. Relinquish the cursing tongue, and refuse to level blame at others for your problems. It does not matter who was responsible. It only matters who will be responsible from this day forward. This is the man or the woman I will work with to bring glory, honor, power, and provisioning. Say within yourself, "My fault and my responsibility," even if you do not think it is fair. For in that humbling of yourself, I will come down and dissolve every fetter, every restriction, every dark strategy of the enemy, and bring you to victory over every foe.

June 1ˢᵗ

Yes, says the Father, unbelievers act foolishly at times. You do not, however, need to remind them because they would not listen to you anyway. They are after all My creation. They seem foolish and, in fact, are foolish because they have not learned not to take themselves seriously. The sobriety of a man often reflects the insecurity that plagues his heart. They have no joy, and they experience no happiness because they fear what they cannot control in their lives. Unbelievers saddle their ego and mount their pride and dash forth in a campaign to control and to conform everyone in their lives to their image and expectations. You know exactly who I am speaking of this day.

Just remember this: I have not called you to negotiate with those in your life with deafened ears and blinded eyes. Leave them alone. Bless them and pray that they will come to a spiritual perception of the world around them. The day will come when you will lovingly embrace even the most bristly enemy once they have seen themselves through My eyes.

Follow what you see the Father do, obey My voice, and patiently endure the consequences of that obedience. Your obedience is the harbinger of My blessing that you have been asking for of late. Blessing will come, and it will not tarry because you have begun to see yourself through My eyes. Therefore, know My joy, My peace, and My provisioning for the challenge you are up against today.

June 2nd

You are invited to be a part of the "great compelling," says the Father. The angels are setting the stage, and My Spirit is convicting hearts. The reaping is for the laborers, and the laborers are for the reaping. See, I have placed the sickle in your hand. It is not a reaping of judgments, but it is a reaping of souls into My garner. The upheaval of nations and the instability in the earth's weather patterns have brought a great questioning in the earth.

I have placed the response of heaven in your heart. I am a God of demonstration for only the demonstration of My Kingdom breaks the hearts of men and women and brings them to the Cross. All else is talk, vanity, and religious foolishness. Press in, says the Father, to demonstration, and I will make known My Spirit and My power as I come alongside you in the work of the great compelling. Will you take your part? The angels have set the stage. My Spirit has convicted and prepared hearts as never before. It is your privilege to participate in the reaping. Open your mouth, open your hand, open your heart, and speak. I will confirm your speaking with corresponding signs, miracles, and wonders that will answer every skeptic, silence every mocker, and win the hearts of loved ones and strangers alike to My Kingdom.

June 3rd

I have digitized My nature this day into your very DNA, says the Father. It is the shed blood of My Son that applies itself to your most basic nature and purges all corruption, pollution, and decay. From the very marrow of My being, My angels of God descended and ascended the ladder I revealed to Jacob at Bethel.

That very sacred place, says the Father, is not located merely in the Middle East, but rather, it is within you even this very moment. As your worship ascends to Me, My nature flows to you and into you. In that transaction you will find My power, My presence, and My potential manifesting in your life. This is the timelessness of My eternal life permeating the time-bound experience in which you live on this earth. I have given you dominion over it and allowed you (by your prayers and your faith-filled decrees) to rule and to reign over your earth--your natural life.

Open your mouth wide, says the Father, and I will fill it. I will fill it with an inward effervescent fullness that will break out of your spiritual belly and overflow every aspect of your life with My blessing, My favor, and the character of My Kingdom. This is your heritage and your inheritance at My hand this day, says the Father.

June 4th

If you seek My face, says the Father, you will see My hand. My hand has not been idle in your life; neither has it worked contrary to your blessing. There have been those who have misrepresented My hand in the earth. They have attributed every calamity, mishap, and disaster to My doing. They have fundamentally misunderstood My nature and have fostered false notions about My character that constitute an accusation against the Cross.

My hand, says the Father, will only produce in the earth what was paid for on the Cross. The suffering of the Cross was not needed to bring about what some have called redemptive suffering in the lives of man. If man must suffer redemptively, then the Cross was unnecessary.

The Cross came to contravene and overturn the very foundations of human nature that cause suffering, sorrow, and lack. The Cross actuates life and life more abundantly--abundance of favor, abundance of provision, abundance of joy, and abundance of liberty from every bondage and fetter. This is what I paid for and what awaits you at My hand.

Seek My face. I will be found of those who seek Me. Seek Me in your meditations, seek Me in your quiet moments. Seek Me in your prayers, your declarations, your worship, and even seek Me in your every ambient thought as you go about your day. In that seeking, says the Father, I will come and visit you with the stroke of My hand and bring forth the very things that you have been petitioning Me for this day.

June 5th

My sound has gone forth from the heavens, says the Father. The enemy of your life is writhing on the earth with his hands over his ears trying to shut out My sound. My voice as the trumpet blast of Glory, melts the heavens, and echoes down into your life. I am that "I am" is reverberating through the days of your life from your distant past to the very last moment of your future on this ball of dust. It is a sound of blessing! It is a declaration of favor! It is a herald of My goodness, My love, and My determinate resolution to bring you to dominion, power, and glory.

As My sound goes forth into all your earth, it causes all that I am in you and through you to fluoresce with My glory and My nature. The enemy looks at you and sees Me. You open your mouth, and He hears My voice coming out! He is confused and disturbed. For as you are clothed in My glory this day, the enemy cannot find a basis to lay claim to that which is yours for I have expunged his every foothold, his every purchase upon your nature, says the Father. You are impregnable to his attack.

So UP! Let us be going! Sally forth and lay claim to every border and every boundary of the captives around you. Let the ring of liberty peal forth from your lips and say, "The captives shall go free!" I would not that your liberty be a solitary blessing. I give you power this day to give away to others what I have activated even this moment in your own life. In the activating as you declare My glory and favor to others, you will experience even greater freedom and provisioning in your own life.

June 6th

I am overturning the works of the enemy in your life today. There is a particular strategy he has used to keep you confined and limited that I am uprooting today. You will feel the pressure. You will sense the turbulence. Fear not. The end result is liberty in areas of your life where you have been bound and stifled.

I will not have you silenced, says the Father. Your laughter is music to My heart. The joy of My Spirit is cascading down upon you. Things are going to get a little topsy-turvy today. Fear not. The enemy will rage and threaten, but I hold the enemy of your soul in derision when he threatens you. I laugh, says the Father, when the enemy accuses you. He reminds me of your failure, and I remind him of his successes. What is the success of the enemy of your soul? He has succeeded in showing you just how inept, incompetent, and unable he is to corrupt, pollute, or destroy your life.

Rejoice, says the Father, and do not allow the sense of spiritual vertigo to cause you to be alarmed. I am overturning and shaking out all the sediments and fragments of the dark one's strategies against you that you might today walk in greater liberty and rejoicing and celebration of life!

June 7th

Sorrow of heart is not the natural state of the believer, says the Father. You will visit there from time to time since it is a fact of life on the earth. In the process you will feel My comfort and My abiding companionship. I will bring you through to a wholesome conclusion for I will not have your life defined by that which you have suffered a loss.

In Christ, says the Father, life is not about loss or bereavement.

There is nothing you have suffered the loss of that I will not recompense and restore. Do you believe this, or do you believe what the circumstance says or what the empty chair says or what the employer said, or the banker, or the lender?

There are many things in life that the enemy would use to cause you to live in devastation and grief. I took those grieves upon Myself that you might walk free from the sting of sorrow. Be comforted today, says the Father. Take your rest, and I will cause your sleep to be sweet. On the morrow take the measurement of the burden that weighs you down this day. Will it not feel just a bit lighter than the day before? Yes, and right speedily, says the Father, for I will cause you to fly again and to mount up into the loftiest places with Me. Trust Me and know that I am He that recompenses and restores the most egregious of losses in your life.

June 8th

I would that you and I are on speaking terms, says the Father. I have a voice, and I have given you ears to hear My words regarding the very minutiae of your least concerns. I will do nothing in your life that is not subject to negotiation because I long for and desire communion and communication with you. Your words ascending to Me are the prompts that cause My words to descend in return to you. My words are not void of power. As My words light upon you, they bring change, healing, and deliverance for you and for those you are connected to in your life.

Being on speaking terms with Me is not the norm among the sons of men, says the Father. Men and women allow their lives to be filled with the cacophony of mindless drivel from many dubious and outward sources. They cannot hear Me above the din of their own thoughts and the bombardment of opinion from without. Yet, there are moments even today if you will quiet yourself that I will inject My articulate heart into your day, and you will experience change and hope and healing.

Tune into Me, and tune out the drone from without. Tune out that which is external, and attune your ear to My voice within. My voice is My Kingdom. When My Kingdom comes, your answers come. Hear My voice today, says the Father. It is the communiqué of My love for you.

June 9th

There are many "love words" that will pass between you and Me, says the Father. They express My heart and My passion for you. One word that will be used frequently is the love word "no." No is a protective word and is a word of comfort from the heart of a Father to the apple of His eye. Have you ever heard it? It is often accompanied by its companion word "never."

"No, I will never forsake you."
"No, I will never abandon you."
"No, I will never allow the pressures of life to overwhelm and destroy you."

Is that what you expected? I have many such words that comprise the vocabulary of My love for you. Let us consider the word "yes." It is accompanied at times as well by the word "often."

"Yes, I will often speak to you in the acoustics of your spirit."
"Yes, I will often use dreams in the night to communicate the mysteries of Glory to you."
"Yes, I will often come to you in the most subtle ways, seeking intimacy throughout your day."

I am always speaking, says the Father. I am ever communing with you. My daily embrace is made up of My words and My communications. Receive My love today, and it will guide you, instruct you, protect you, and provision you for the challenges of the day.

June 10th

Arrogance does not serve your enemy well, says the Father. Your enemy thinks he has the upper hand. He thinks he has cut you off from every avenue of escape or deliverance. He thinks he has rendered your prayers inert and dashed your hopes. I have taken all this into account and have pondered his audacity against you with growing wrath, says your Father.

I am come down to end this strategy of hell against you. I will depose the dark one and vanquish all his tacticians. They have thought to surround you with snares, assaults, and attacks, but I am defending you. From the lightning and thunder of My throne room, there is coming a sound of deliverance. Can you hear it? Can you hear My sound? Perhaps you can echo this sound with Me. It is best that you are looking the enemy directly in the face when you do this, says the Father.

Bah, ha, ha!

I will have him in derision. I will cause the smoke of the enemy's destruction to rise up before your face, and you will rejoice at what My hands have wrought on your behalf.

Laugh, says the Father. Laugh the laugh of faith. The enemy hates that mockery. The laugh of faith keeps him awake nights because he knows that the laugh of faith in your mouth is the harbinger of his immanent destruction!

June 11th

Abiding in the vine is not an option for those who purpose to ascend in Me. I would rather that you walk in the ascension life of the vine, says the Father. As you ascend in worship, you shall descend in warfare. Worship is the precursor to warfare against the enemy of your soul.

Worship is an act of ascension to My throne where the vine is rooted and gives forth His life. I invite you today to participate in My vine life, says the Father. When you manifest vine life, that life that is in you will cause you (as the vine) to surmount every wall and pull down every tree that I have not planted. Ascend in the vine today, says the Father. Ascend in Me. Allow Me to extend My di-VINE-ity to you and through you for therein is the VINE-tage that you seek in My Spirit!

June 12th

I am auditing the plantings in your life today, says the Father.

You will even sense the scrutiny in the morning time, but I do not want you to be in trepidation. Remember that I am the personification of love. Love is who I am, and it is what I do. There are plantings in your life and things that have root and branch that are not of My doing, says the Father. I will be speaking to those things (those relationships, circumstances, and settings), and they will begin to whither almost instantly.

I am extracting some things out of your circumstance from which you are, in fact, emotionally invested. Fear not, for I have not called you to merely be an emotional being but to be a spiritual being in Me. I gave you the ability to be attached to people, places, and things, but I do not intend that your capacity for attachment be a means by which the dark one brings you into emotional captivity.

When you see the withering of things you are emotionally anchored in, says the Father, say within yourself, "I will set my affections above (where Christ sits at the right hand of God) and not on things of the earth." In so doing you will deliver yourself from the Babylonian confusion that has for too long impeded the fullness of My blessing in your life.

Yes, I am auditing your life today, says the Father. Rejoice, for the emptying that comes is only the clearing out of space and time so that I might fill you with better promises.

June 13th

What is the price of victory, says the Father? Sacrifice is the work of Calvary and the primary purview of My Son in the earth. The death I have called you to is the death of the Son that you might be a partaker of His resurrection.

Do you understand that I place no premium upon human suffering? I know that is not what you have been taught. They have called every vile crisis, tragedy, and disaster an "act of God." Even those who speak in My name have enshrined in your life the very things My Son died to remove from your experience. He died so that you might live. He took stripes so that you might be healed. He was rejected and despised so that you might be accepted and approved. He even became poor that you might by rich (the very coinage in your purse that cankers with age and is spent and gone tomorrow made a substitutionary provision). He had no place to lay His head so that you might have the roof that I have provided.

Put your faith in Me and not in those who indict My character with their blathering about the "mysterious purposes of God." My purpose is this:

That you might live
That you might have health
That you might have provision
That you might be blessed and highly favored in all aspects of life that the cross of My Son redresses

Put your confidence in Me, says the Father, and open your hand for I am about to fill you with every good thing beginning today.

June 14th

Compromise is not in the vocabulary of the Kingdom, says the Father. You do not have to relinquish one dream, one desire, or one heart's cry of that which I have encoded into your very being. You do not have to settle for less than what My Son paid for on the Cross. It is in My plan this day and every day till the end of your sojourning that you get the full benefit of all that was paid for by the cross of Christ. Expect it and ask Me for it.

Requisition heaven, and angels of the throne will stamp the purchase order "paid in full by the shed blood of Calvary." Yes, it is true you have gotten yourself into much of the mess you are facing today. Do you not realize that is the universal human condition? When I made the provision of Calvary, I took into account your personal capacity to ruin your own life and rob yourself of My blessing.

Be forgiven, says the Father. Forgive yourself for the foolishness of your own wrong choices in life. From the ashes of disappointment and loss, I am forming a habitation of joy, peace, and rest. Come unto

Me, and lay your head on Daddy's shoulder. I have everything under control, and all is well!

June 15th

My deep is calling to your deep today, says the Father. My voice echoes beyond the din and hue of the hectic environment from which you are surrounded. My voice resonates in the deepest chambers of your innermost being. My voice is calling! My Spirit is longing to release to you My heart and My mind.

My voice is calling you to relinquish the urgent and lay hold on the importance of spending time with Me. In so doing My mind will stretch itself over your mind as Elijah stretched himself upon the dead lad in times of old. I will bring you to new life. I will open your eyes that you might see there are more that be for you than those that be against you. I will cause you to understand with My great understanding how you might flow with and cooperate with My purposes.

The exhaustion and weariness which plagues you at times results from a lack of understanding My dealings in your life on a day-to-day basis. With all your desire to know Me and to know My ways, you often set yourself at cross-purposes with what I am doing. Relax, says the Father. The current of your life is guided by My hand. Let Me take you on and take you deeper into Me, and you will see all the urgent, demanding, threatening circumstances will weary themselves of finding the door of access to do any actual damage to your life.

Do you trust Me? Let Me take it from here. Come away. Come away, My beloved. Release your deep to My deep, and commune with Me in the uncharted waters of My Spirit.

June 16th

Today I am leading you by the streams of gladness, says the Father. I placed these waters in your path for your own particular use. I created you to need and receive refreshing from time to time. My Spirit is the refreshment intended for your renewal and cleansing. You may access these waters in many ways. They all involve taking your attention off things that do not really matter and be eclipsed by My love and My passion for you.

Would you like to take a drink? You could wade in and splash around, says the Father. Go ahead--I invite you! I love to watch My children play. Perhaps you might want to plunge in and be immersed in My presence. Maybe you are one that would go so far out in My presence that the shoreline of earthly things is no longer there for a frame of reference.

Yes, you can lose yourself in Me. Do not be afraid. I will sustain you. I am the current underneath you and the river around you. I am taking you further and deeper into Myself. There is nothing in My presence that will harm or diminish you. Out here is where the angels play. Go ahead, let your "self" go, and plunge deeper into Me!

June 17th

The secret of living in the supernatural is to lean into Me. Depending on natural resources, talent, and conventional wisdom will anchor you to the earthly. All earthly things decay and garner disappointment, says the Father. I would not have your hopes dashed or your dreams unrealized. Lean into Me. Cast yourself with abandon against the impossibilities that face you today. You will know Me as the God of the impossible as you hurl yourself (body, soul, and spirit) against the towering challenges of your life on a daily basis.

You have asked Me for miracles, and miracles are on the way to you. The miracle is there and will manifest as you work in cooperation with Me. I will cause your miracle to emerge and manifest in your moment of desperation. Yes, says the Father, I will change minds, I will change hearts, I will change physical circumstances, and even change bank balances for I am a twenty-first-century God, who will do miracles in a twenty-first-century world.

Do not look back at 2000 years ago and wonder, says the Father. No, look at the "here and now" for I am showing up in your life today, and you will no longer be speaking of what I did long ago or what I did in someone else's life. You will testify of Me and rejoice in all your "todays" for I am a "right-now God" bringing a "right-now deliverance" to your life and your situation!

June 18th

I turned the captivity of Job when he prayed for his friends, says the Father. What do you propose that I do for you when you follow the same example? Write it down even now, says the Father. Is there anything too hard for Me? You have asked and asked Me more than once. Now is the time to ask on behalf of your friends.

I will move in your life as you pray and petition Me for a manifestation of deliverance on behalf of those you call your peers. It is true that many of them have not been friends in the truest sense, but leave that to Me. There are answers they are crying out for to which they will never receive until you pray, says the Father.

Will you deny them their answers at My hand? I did not think so. Ask largely on their behalf. Ask boldly. Ask audaciously. Ask for the very things you know they are struggling for faith to receive. As your faith extends itself like a delivering wind over your peers, says the Father, look behind you! Out of the shadows of unrealized dreams and visions, I am about to parade a caravan of blessing into your life.

This is how it works, says the Father. As you pray for others, your own dreams are realized. Not understanding this is why many have languished in sorrow (not knowing and not understanding). They even concluded that I simply was not willing to answer their prayers. They thought I was neglecting them like they were neglecting to pray for others. Strange that the Cross did not speak to that contradiction they supposed existed in My character.

Faith is working, says the Father. It is working by love, and it is bringing My power to bear on all those you lift up to Me today. It is working by love to deliver to your door the very answers you are seeking.

June 19ᵗʰ

There is a piercing taking place in your life today, says the Father. It is an intrusion and an inconvenience. Your first reaction would be to put your hand on it and deal swiftly with the problem. I say to you--wait! I will deal with the source of this pain and keep you from the snare that the enemy has laid in your path.

The dark one has taken notice that you have drawn your eye away from him and what he is doing. He realizes that you have turned your attention upon Me and upon My Kingdom. He said in his counsels, "We can't have this. How do we snare this one and bring him/her back to an earthbound limitation?" He purposes are to do so by a stinging attack. Do not give in to it, says the Father.

I am sending reinforcements to the angels already assigned on your behalf. You will sense them and know you are not alone in the fight. Do not take matters into your own hands. Resist evil. Wait upon My voice to direct you in what you will do and what you will say. If you follow Me in this, says the Father, at the end of the day the dark one will be pouting over his failure to harm you, and you will be smiling and rejoicing at how good it is to be in tune with the Father and protected by His hand.

June 20ᵗʰ

Drink from My Spirit today, says the Father. As you rise today, My paternity is activated on the inside of you. Let who I am and what I am rise up and clothe your every conscious thought. Allow who I am to overshadow your very self-awareness. I created you to be God-conscious. When man fell, his self-consciousness eclipsed his awareness of Me. I began to change that when I sent My Son to provide new birth. Be a follower of Me as a dear child, and imitate Me today.

You are asking in the circumstances you face today, "What am I going to do?" Allow your spirit to instruct your soul and say, "We will do what our Father would do if He was in our shoes!" Because I am in you and I am expressing My personhood in you in the face of all your challenges, demand your life to respond to you even as I demanded the formless void to respond to My voice in the beginning. We have wonderful things ahead for you, says the Father, as you walk in My personhood and lay claim to My paternity in your heart.

June 21st

The Father says that you should monitor the weather of your spirit. As you go low and worship, the rains of favor and blessing you are asking for will come. Going low in worship brings the bright clouds of anointing, favor, and blessing. Choosing humility will alter the spiritual environment of your life. It will end the dry season, and it will bring forth fruitfulness and harvest.

Alternatively, when you take matters into your own hands and seek to solve your crises in your own strength, the result is stagnation and pressure. Go low, says the Father, and the heavens will open. An open heaven is no secret. An open heaven will automatically manifest over you as you satisfy the conditions of relinquishing and rest that bring My favor, my blessing, and my anointing to bear on every aspect of your life.

Are you ready for a downpour? Have you been wondering when the dry spell would end? The Spirit of God is in the ascendency when your will is in abeyance. My Spirit will refresh, rebuild, and restore as you relinquish your will and yield to My promise in your life. Go ahead-- the blessing is waiting. It is ready to be poured out of the bright clouds that have formed over you even as you have heard this admonition.

June 22nd

I am replacing your weariness with joy, says the Father. I am activating inside of you my irreducible life. The reserves you are drawing on today cannot be capped; their capacity is limitless. The resources I am opening to you are unbounded and limitless. Draw upon Me today for all your needs.

As your praise is verbally articulated, it reaches My courts and unleashes the waiting deliveries of grace, joy, provision, protection, and wisdom, says the Father. Your praise and your worship looses in heaven those blessings that are laid in store, awaiting the occasion of your faith. Is there anything too hard for Me?

What would you have Me do for you today? You are going to have to ask Me. The spiritual reserves by which I uphold the universe traverse the earth for you on the resonant, audible strains of your prayers. Pray expansively, says the Father. Ask largely. Expect greatly for I am doing more than you can ask or think.

June 23rd

The Father says today to continue in My love. When you continue in love, you are continuing in Me because love is who I am. Love is not simply what I do, but it is the actual strata of My constituent nature. This is why I never fail to love, and it is why My love is without respect of person. I love you because I love you. I will never stop loving you. I love you, and there is nothing you can do about it! You are loved.

When you continue in love (because love is who I am), you are continuing in My limitlessness. This is why faith works by love. Choosing to love brings Me intimately on the scene of your greatest need. When I show up in your choice to love, it is in the nature of My character to meet every need, solve every problem, deliver every captive, and make every provision.

You have wondered at times where I was in the situation. I declare to you, says the Father, I am always there. You often ask me, "When will you manifest your glory?" I will manifest My power in the very moment that you allow the love that I am to be the love that you are in with every interaction and every situation. Today, says the Father, allow My limitlessness to be expressed through you. The walls will come down, the problems will be solved, and the answers you are crying out for will be made manifest.

June 24th

I will make an end, says the Father. I will make an end to your suffering and to your dry season with the breaking of the morning. I have seen your struggle. I have seen and I am moved with compassion in your behalf. In My compassion I will make a difference. I will make a difference between daylight and darkness in your life, and I will bring an end to the attacks of the enemy. I will lift the heavy burden you are struggling under this day. I place no premium on human suffering, says the Father. Receive this day the tally of that which the Cross provided. I am clearing your path, and I will make a way for you where there seems to be no way. Despair not, and do not let the hands that are weary hang down. No, lift up those hands in surrender to My care for you.

Do you trust Me? Then, let me take it from here. For now is the day of deliverance, and now is the very moment of your relief. You will lay your head on the pillow this night, and your last thought before blessed sleep will be, "Father, you do all things well!"

June 25th

I have not called you to be a barnyard believer, says the Father. I have called you to soar with Me above the prattle and cackling of the earth-minded crowd. The ruling and reigning I have destined you for will never be implemented until you opt out of the pecking order of men.

There are those surrounding you who understand that success and blessing is only contrasted by their ability to take unfair advantage of others. This is not to be your portion. Let the complaints of men and their incessant grumbling drone on, says the Father. Pay no heed to their growling and jostling against you and one another.

Look upward, away from natural concerns and competitiveness, and fasten your attention upon Me. You are where your attention takes you. Up here with Me in the heavens is the feast and the table that I have prepared for you. Just walk away from the scraps that others are fighting to acquire. Let them have their pound of flesh. You are destined for the throne, and it is there you will rule and reign with Me over all the affairs of life.

Speak My Word in your solitude of prayer, and I will dispatch the angelic hosts to bring My words in your mouth to pass and cause My Kingdom to come, bringing order out of the chaos that lies before you now.

June 26th

I am drawing your roots deep into Me, says the Father. When all other sources of supply have left men withered and empty, you will yet be vibrant, green, and fruitful. My deep is calling to your deep, and there is more to you than meets the eye. Your foundations are in Me, and I will sustain you.

The resources you are crying out for will not come as "pennies from heaven." Your treasure in Me is at your feet. You will access the glory by the decree of your lips. Yes, says the Father, even today you will decree a thing, and it will rise up before you: decree provision; decree restoration; and decree healing and deliverance. Make bold your decree, and I will make haste to bring it to pass. Resolve within your heart to abandon all those weak prayers. Weak prayers never make it out of the gravity-well of earthly things, says the Father. Pray boldly! Pray audaciously! Pray like there is no tomorrow! I do not live in the tomorrows, says the Father. I live in your eternal now.

Fret not. Do not be dismayed at the current chaos and burdensome situation. Fretfulness does not move the mountain! Speak to the burdens that are neither easy nor light in your life, and command them to "step off." You will be amazed at the authority I have invested in your words. I will answer, and I will answer speedily, says the Father, as you cooperate with Me in your mouth and in your faith-filled decrees.

June 27th

I will not leave you wounded, says the Father. I am not overlooking your pain or your suffering. Even as those around you may choose to politely skirt the issues that pain you most, I am going directly to the heart of the matter. I am reaching in by My hand to extract the putrefaction that has festered in your life, and I am removing it and pouring in the astringent cleansing of My Spirit.

Trust Me to heal, to mend, and to recover you at this deepest level. Do not snatch yourself away when I get closer than you can stand to those most intimate, painful wounds. Trust Me. I have shared those wounds. I have taken them by way of the Cross, returning in their place the resurrection life. I am exchanging your struggle for My rest, and I am exchanging your shame for My cleansing.

I am imparting to you My strength today that you might know there is nothing I will leave undone in your life and nothing of importance to you that I will ignore or fail to address. This is the day things begin to get better, says the Father. Expect it. Believe for it. Rejoice in the recovery for the time has come!

June 28th

I am hiding you in My pavilion today, says the Father. I am sheltering you under My wings. Under the shadow of My wings is your oft-abiding place. It is there I nurture you, and it is there I bathe you in the intimacy of My presence. In My presence you shall find solace till the bluster and blowing of the storms of strife and calamity are past. In the final analysis man can take nothing from you that cannot be restored by My hand.

I am more than enough for this day's challenges! I am sufficient to meet every cry of your heart. Adapt yourself and your thinking to My limitlessness. My unlimited ability is tied to My unbridled love for you. In that love I am sheltering, providing, protecting, and consoling you this day, says the Father.

June 29th

The Father says, My signs are great in you! My wonders are mighty in you! My Kingdom in you is everlasting. My dominion in you and My sovereignty in you is from generation to generation. I am transmuting My sovereignty to your generation that you might rule and reign with Me in the earth. Did you think you would necessarily wait for heaven before you would rule and reign? I will not put down spiritual wickedness in high places without using you as the instrumentality through which I do it.

Receive this day not just My sovereignty in your life but My sovereignty over your life. I have given you the regency to deploy My might, My signs, and My wonders against the ramparts of the dark one that would attempt to limit and confine you to a merely human existence.

You are not merely human! You are infused with My life. The DNA of My Spirit courses through your veins by virtue of the propitiation of the blood-bought provisions of the Cross. Do not trust in yourself. Trust in who I am on the inside of you. Trust that the provisions of 2000 years ago are the "now experience provision" to put you over in the situation you are facing today.

June 30th

Saddle Me with your cares today, says the Father. Throw down against Me all of those things that distract you and keep you awake at night. Cast them away with gusto! Cast them with vehemence for I will have you without care. I would have you careful for nothing.

You are the object of My concern, says the Father. You are not a side issue in My Kingdom. There are no trivial, unimportant matters or issues in My heart regarding you. Over every problem and challenge, I am providing necessary superintendence and timely assistance. Expect deliverance. Expect healing. Expect provisioning. Expect victory over every obstacle.

Cast all your cares upon Me today and be carefree! Go ahead! I dare you, says the Father. I have got this, and I am not pacing the floor before My throne or wringing My hands wondering what I am going to do. This crisis in your life did not catch Me by surprise or cause Me to push the panic button. There is no panic in My Kingdom. Look to the deliverance that I am issuing toward you even now. Proscribe (banish) the parameters of that deliverance with the faith-filled decrees of your mouth. Today is the day that I make all the difference in your life.

July 1st

I am the God of the struggle, says the Father. Struggle is not negative or outside the parameters of the "Kingdom experience." The struggles in life that you face are opportunities I have allowed by My hand. They are opportunities for you to flex your "dominion muscles." I have encoded the quest for dominion on the inside of you. I have placed within you the natural tendency to walk into the situations of life and engulf them with the resources of heaven that I have imbued you with from before you were born.

I have given you life and life more abundantly. When you retire from the struggle, that is the spirit of death at work--death to your dreams, death to your hopes, and death itself. I would have you charge the pickets of the enemy of your soul today and take back the promises and provisions I gave you that he is trying to steal!

Yes, there are weapons of enmity formed against you today. There are problems (big problems) out there just waiting to swallow you. But, I have made provision for you to steamroll the dark one and overcome in victory!

Rejoice, smile, laugh, and even giggle, says the Father. Open your mouth, and declare a brazen decree that you are not going under. You are going over! I will not allow your life to be defined by loss or devastation. This is not the end of anything; it is the beginning of your new-found fruitfulness.

July 2nd

I am reflecting Myself in you today, says the Father. True evangelism is not processed through the mind or from your thoughts to the thoughts of another. I am a God of demonstration; therefore, mere words are ancillary to the purpose of revealing My glory. I am not establishing in your life today a repository of religious verbiage but a demonstration of My power and My glory. Are you ready?

There are adjustments I will initiate in your person as I act to clarify Myself in you. Christ in you will be in evidence. At the same time the natural mind and thoughts that have clouded My character in you will begin to recede. You are the chalice of My presence, says the Father. When I look in your heart, I see the Lamb slain from the foundation of the world. When the dark one looks, he sees the Lion of Judah, and he trembles.

I have no other choice than to see you this way, and the dark one has no choice than to see you this way. The only ones who actually have a choice as to what they see in you are yourself and others. What do you see when you look in the mirror, says the Father? I would like you see the lamb nature and the lion authority. In that authority I commission you today (this very hour) to go forth and begin to superintend your life according to the dictates and promises of My Word.

Command the storm to be still! Command the promise to be fulfilled! Command the dark one to depart from your life and the lives of those around you. I am commissioning you even today, says the Father. Do you accept the commission, or are you just a saber rattler? Be bold in Me today. I will not disappoint, and I will not fail to back your words, prayers, and declarations. I am reflecting Myself in you today. Go out and unleash that reflected glory on your world.

July 3rd

I would desire that you live before Me with an unveiled face, says the Father. Only then will the glory be seen that I have placed within you. Pretense and obfuscation (confusion) are inherent in Christian religious cultures. I am releasing you today from those bonds and encouraging you to be yourself with Me and with others.

Moses veiled his face before the people so they would not see his imperfect humanity. Even in the wilderness with water from the rock and manna every morning, the Israelites worshiped the creation rather than the Creator. I am prepared to bring you manna every morning and water from the rock, says the Father. In this season you are entering, the miraculous will be the norm, and you will not know an unanswered prayer. But, you must be "real" with Me and "real" with the people around you, or this time of blessing will be unnecessarily foreshortened.

I will protect you. I will preserve you. I will provision you, says the Father. You will not need to put up walls of separation between yourself and others. Allow who I am and what I am to be made manifest through your naked humanity and vulnerability. My glory will then increase and not fade away as it did in Moses' face.

It is a new day, says the Father. It is a new morning of blessing and the manifestation of My light and life. I invite you to be a participator and a carrier of that light.

July 4th

I am the God who is more than enough, says the Father. I have seen the deficits in your life. I have counted your pennies more times than you have counted them. I have taken notice of every act of belt-tightening and frugality as you have struggled to adjust to your economic situations. Money is no challenge to My ability. Financial problems are not possessed of some unique resistance to My ability to answer prayer.

Ask, says the Father.
Seek, says the Father.
Knock, says the Father.

I will accept your petition, and I will act on your behalf. As I brought supernatural provision to My people in the wilderness, so will I bring answers to your material needs. There is nothing about your life that does not concern Me. I endured poverty, and I had no place to lay My head in My earth walk. This was done on your behalf. I suffered lack that you might receive provisioning by My hand.

Are you ready for change? Call out to Me. Petition My hand. You are going to have to ask Me, and you are going to have to ask with anticipation and trust, knowing that I am receiving your request with compassion and grace. Even this day I am about to make all the difference, says the Father.

July 5th

I invented fun, says the Father. You enjoy diversion and entertainment because you are made in My image. We can have fun together. We can laugh and smile. I created humor and injected it into the character of man for no other reason than to give you pleasure and to enjoy your fellowship.

Do not take yourself too seriously today, says the Father. The dark one would keep you somber and stern-faced in order to dissuade others from My Kingdom. They think My children cannot have any fun; this could not be further from the truth. Having fun with the Father is the sweetest, most productive activity you can know in your walk with Me. As we love and laugh, we also heal and mend, proclaim liberty to the captives, sight to the blind, and proclaim the acceptable year of the Lord. There is no challenge before you today, says the Father, that requires Me or you to become somber and austere.

Smile, says the Father. We are going to have some fun today. Look for Me in the strangest places. Expect Me to do the unusual, the unique, and even that which the religious crowd would claim is out of character for the "God of the universe." They do not know Me. They have got Me all wrong. Come now and let us walk together and enjoy this day that I have prepared just for you.

July 6th

The Father says, I am a fire from My loins upward and My loins downward, and I would cause My fire to burn in the depths of your being today. Make offering today, says the Father, of all that is combustible in your life. I will burn away the chaff, purge the dross, and give you beauty for ashes and the oil of joy for mourning. Those things in your life and in your heart that cannot survive My kindling do not serve your best interest. Serve Me without distraction and without impediment. Even in your little corner of the world, allow the fires of My Spirit to kindle and burn so that I might cause you to shine and manifest My glory.

You are My candle, and you are the lamp of My burning. There is no other chosen receptacle of My glory than that which I am causing you to be this day, says the Father. As you become the ignition source for My glory, the darkness will flee away, and the strategy of the dark one will be exposed.

Exposing the enemy is equivalent with his defeat. You will walk in victory and put your foot in the neck of your enemy (even the enemy of your soul who has panted after your destruction). Put your trust in

Me today. Allow the passion of My Kingdom and for My purposes to direct your every decision as you cast off the bushel basket of convention and timidity and become that light set on a hill which will cause all darkness to hide and My glory to be made manifest to all in your circle.

July 7th

Do you realize it has been given you to know the mysteries of the Kingdom? The wisdom of men withholds, but that is not My choice or My wisdom. I take that which men would prevent and reveal it unto babes. I have chosen you to take custody of the mysteries of the Kingdom, says the Father. Those mysteries have been passed over by illegitimate authority as being "too deep" for you. This is because the mysteries of the Kingdom will break the power that religious spirits hold over you.

Religious spirits bind you and hold you down with guilt and superstition. The mysteries of the Kingdom justify and empower you. Receive My empowerment today. I would like everything you do and say today to become as effective as if I said it and did it. It is your portion to imitate Me. It is your privilege to do what I would do if I were in your position because I am in your position and facing your challenges because I am Christ in you.

I will not leave you comfortless, powerless, or helpless. You are being pressed today, so do something about it. Stand and speak. Stand and declare. Speak and require the elements, the principalities, and even time and happenstance to bend to My glory that is working on your behalf to bless, release, and provision you.

July 8th

The voice of My blood is speaking over you. Abel's blood cried out at his death by the hands of his brother. My blood has been crying out from the Cross for 2000 years. My shed blood has called your name, and it has reverberated through the universe into the very heavens. My blood has a voice, and My Father responds to the voice of My shed blood.

The testimony of My blood is a testimony of your cleansing, your forgiveness, and your victory over every opposition. When the voice of doubt, the voice of the accuser, and the voice of fear raises its objections, the blood shed at Calvary shouts down every contradiction to your blessing, your healing, and your provision. Your role is to synchronize your voice with that redemptive cry, says the Father. Let your voice affirm:

I am forgiven
I am victorious
I am provisioned
I am healed

This day heaven is synchronizing with the earth in your life. This day the inexorable transition from the domain of darkness to the Kingdom of God begins afresh and anew. Expect it. Embrace it. Adjust your expectations to that of one who is walking in Kingdom entitlement for that is your portion today.

July 9th

I have purposed to increase you with the increase you have asked Me for, says the Father. I am not a god of deprivation, and I place no premium upon lack or poverty of spirit. I came that you might have life--irreducible life in abundance. Say within your heart, "I refuse to live below the provisions of Christ! I refuse to live without any favor, any blessing, any provision that Christ has made for me."

There is no deficit, no power in hell, and no force on the earth that can deprive you of that which I have purposed in My Spirit to accord to you. Open your mouth wide like a baby bird, and I will fill you with good things and increase My benefits in your life on a daily basis. Do you believe this? If you fail to believe, you will experience the absence of the very things I paid for by the stripes on My back and the nails in My hands. Stand boldly against the conditions of life that contradict My promise. Speak confidently and pray resolutely. You will receive the full dividends of Calvary in this life and that which is to come.

July 10th

I am not in love with the plan, says the Father. I am in love with you. You are My well-beloved, My intended, My intention, and even as the pupil of My eye. I will never leave you or forsake you. I will never abandon or leave you. I will never choose the good of the plan above what is best for you because the plan of the ages has you at its apex and the height of its fulfillment.

I am the architect of the ages and the columns of time. The ramparts of eternity were formed and fashioned as an expression of My passion for you. There is nothing about you that is infinitesimal in My estimation or a marginal priority to Me. Do you believe this? Then know that I am guiding your life according to My sovereign and determinate purpose. You can trust the plan because you can trust Me. I will not leave you out, and I will not leave any unmet needs or unanswered prayers. In the days ahead I am going to reveal My plan as it relates intimately and personally to you.

Get a pen and journal. Write when I tell you to write. The next five years are crucial, and I am going to paint them before you as an artist paints on a canvas. Hide the things in your heart I tell you to hide. Proclaim the things from the rooftop I tell you to proclaim. You can see this day, says the Father, that you are not just part of the plan--you are the plan--and you are the focus of My determinate purpose.

July 11th

I am establishing you in righteousness, says the Father. I am establishing you in the righteousness that is who I am and what I am.

I am your righteousness.
I am the condition in your heart that causes everything you say and do to become effective as if I said it or did it.

I am the condition in your heart that gives you the favor of heaven before My throne.

I am the condition in your heart that gives you authority before the principalities and powers that are raged against you and set against your life.

I invite you to exercise the reality of who I am in you today. I invite you to unleash who I am against the adversities and challenges in your situation. "Let Me at 'em," says the Spirit of the Lord your God!

I am the God who loves a good fight! I am a God who is a master pugilist (boxer) well able to crush your enemies and turn defeat into victory. I only await the occasion of your verbally articulate, faith-filled prayers to put Me in the ring of competition and ring the opening bell! I am going to win a knock-out blow on your behalf, and you will see it and rejoice that you staked your winnings on the outcome that I am providing today.

July 12th

I am not a far-off God, says the Father. I am as close as the breath in your body. I am more intimate with you than your innermost thoughts. I am available. I am accessible. I am motivated by the cries of your heart to bring about that change.

Outward circumstances reflect inward conditions. As the internal atmosphere of My Kingdom within you gains ground in your soul, the outward pressures will begin to yield to My blessings. I would have you prosper and be in health even as your soul prospers.

I place no premium upon human suffering (and that includes you). I take no pleasure in your humiliation and find no higher, inscrutable purpose in the imposition of lack, poverty, sorrow, or sickness upon you. Those who have taught otherwise have failed to give My Word the ascendancy in their thinking. I am not intimidated by your failures. I am not put off by your shortcomings. When you were at your worst, I looked upon you and made estimation of you that called for the sacrifice of the Cross.

Are you ready to change your mind? Are you ready to think like I think, speak like I speak, and act like I act? My patience is enduring, but there are opportunities that will pass you by unnecessarily unless you relinquish your guilt-ridden, religiously structured thinking. Be an imitator of Me today. Let My thoughts guide you. Let My Word counsel you. Let My power encompass you today, says the Father, and you will see new blessing and fresh winds of My Spirit.

July 13th

I am turning up the heat in your life, says the Father. The fires of My Spirit are touching every combustible thing in your path until only that which is of eternal value is shining forth. The enemy has sought to clutter your life and impede your destiny with distractions. This day I will act against that strategy by My hand. Say within your heart this day:

> I will only do what I see My Father do.
> I will only say what I hear My Father say.
> I will make every decision by My Father's hand.

In so doing you will cooperate with My delivering hand and deposit yourself in the very heart of My Kingdom in your life. My government is increasing in the earth, and you are a part of it. I will not pass you by, and I will not leave you behind. We are going to conquer together and bring forth victory unto righteousness, says the Father.

July 14th

You have a secret weapon in your arsenal, says the Father. Against it the enemy is totally defenseless. It is the condition of a contrite and a humble heart. I give grace (My empowering presence to the humble); however, I set even My forces in array against the proud.

The assaults you are facing today will be deflected and defused as you make a conscious choice to go low and worship. Do you really want to keep fighting the battle in your own strength? Has this not proved untenable and exhausting? Has anything changed or gotten better?

Lean into Me, says the Father. Find shelter and solace in My presence. My presence is with you as you go through your day. Know that I am by your side, provisioning you with My empowering presence.

I will repair the irreparable. I will mend the unmendable. I will provision you, protect you, and give you peace this day, says the Lord your God.

July 15th

There is nothing uncommon about the stresses you face today, says the Father. The enemy would have you believe that your situation is uniquely difficult and unsolvable, but that is a lie from the father of lies. You are possessed within My irreducible life. I planted My life within you before the foundation of the ages. When I went to the Cross, that life was activated on your behalf. When you accepted My covenantal relationship, all that the Cross affords was activated on the inside of you as a resource to address every need, every obstacle, and every challenge.

As you face the difficulties of the day, take action to deploy heaven's resources against the strategies of the dark one. I will not have you impoverished. I will not have you in sickness. I will not allow you to live in despair. Take flight in Me by the verbal release and inward confidence in My words and My promises. This is a day of days for you, says the Father. This day will be a receipt of the purchase price of heaven. This day is a packet of heavenly experience and blessing so you will know and have a foretaste of what awaits in the eternities.

July 16th

What are you lacking today, says the Father? Do you remember what I told Peter? He was more intimidated by his tax debt than he was impressed by my ability to provide. I sent him to cast a hook into the sea, and he found the fish with a silver coin in its mouth.

I have many, many "silver-coin discoveries" for you in your walk with Me, says the Father. You do not need to do anything other than simply hear My voice, go where I send you, and do what I tell you. Where you have a need will present itself as you respond to My voice. It is not magic. It is not as some have accused Me--the "carrot and stick" proposition. The silver coin adventures are simply hearing, obeying, and experiencing what happens in My Kingdom when your hear and obey.

What is your silver coin challenge today? What are you needing—healing, relationship restoration, or actual material provisions? You are going to have to ask Me, but do not stop there. Having asked Me and having heard My response, you must then obey! Go where I send you, and do what I tell you. Are you ready to have some fun and miracles?

July 17th

Have you ever contemplated the fact that I am a "yes" God? I have said yes to you in order that you might have authority to say "no" to the dark one (the enemy of your soul). All of My promises are "yes," says the Father. The death on the Cross ratified My promises, and the resurrection validated My ability to make good on those promises.

I will never say no to those things I have promised. Once promised, when you come to ask of Me, I do not lean back on the throne and ponder, "Will I make good on My word today?" It is not about how good you are because you are not good, and you are not worthy to have one prayer answered (that is, in your own worth), says the Father.

Once petitioned, I do not look at your life to see if you have been "naughty or nice." I do not wear a red coat with a long white beard! Once I have been asked, I look to the righteousness of Christ at My right hand. I answer your petitions based on My promise and My provision of righteousness through Christ Jesus. Waver not, says the Father. Let there not be that nagging doubt that I would ever deny you one promise found in My Word.

Ask! Ask that your joy might be full! Ask that I might fill your heart with joy and your house with laughter. In the asking is your victory and your provisioning, says the Father, for your asking looses the silver cords of heaven's provisions and brings them into your life as life-giving rain!

July 18th

Do not let good doctrines in your head put a damper on the seed of faith in your heart, says the Father. It is not important that you theologically understand how I will answer your prayer; it is only important that you know I will answer your prayer.

Always pray in simplicity. Do not change the tone of your voice or speak to Me with some ancient vocabulary as though that is necessary to be heard. And, do not pray out how you want Me to answer. Leave the details to me!

I am a God of creativity. I delight in "wowing" you with how I am going to do what you have asked of Me. (Pardon Me, says the Father, if I do not check with the learned theologians to make sure My sovereign deliverance on your behalf measures up with their tinder dry, dead-doctrinal suppositions about who I am and what I will do in any given circumstance.) Ask in faith, and leave the details to Me. Pray the answer and not the problem. Pray the outcome and not the process.

Relax and live in your now. I will let you know if I need your help being the sovereign God of the universe in your life today! Isn't that a chuckle? Smile, says the Father. You know you have tried to help Me be God occasionally. This is not about you helping Me be the Father—it is about Me helping you be My dear children. So rejoice, relax, and leave the answers to Me. I am about to change everything in your life if you will simply and audaciously look to Me for your deliverance.

July 19th

Occasionally, says the Father, I will show up in your life in a way that you have never experienced. When I walked on the water toward My disciples in the boat, they were afraid and thought I was a demon spirit! You will see Me coming and see evidence of something taking place, but you will not be sure if it is Me or the work of the enemy. Fear not! I will always certify My hand in your life with the inward assurance, "Fear not, it is I!"

Adjust your thinking and accept that I am a God of mystery and sovereignty. There are prayers you are praying right now that require I take you outside your comfort zone and out past (way out past) your current understanding. The only way out of your comfort zone is "on the waves and waters!" I am with you, so enjoy the trip. When you are terrified and wondering if you made a great mistake, just relax and remind yourself that you are going to have a great testimony by the time it is all done.

July 20th

What authority do you suppose you will have in eternity that you do not have right now, says the Father? I say to you that all authority in heaven and earth is given to the Son. All that the Son has been given was transferred upon you 2000 years ago.

Ruling and reigning does not begin in some future time. Ruling and reigning begins now. You are a principality and a power at this present time. I hold heaven and earth and every created thing accountable to the faith-filled words of My people. There is no legitimate rule in the earth that supersedes your prayers, your intercessions, or your declarations and decrees.

The strategy of the enemy is to put you on the defensive and keep you in the great unknowing. However, Christ in you is standing up in the temple (the temple you are even this day). Be followers and be imitators of Me, says the Father. Do what I would do if I were in your circumstance, and I will call heaven's resources to bring you forth in deliverance, provision, power, and victory over every obstacle in your way, says the Lord your God.

July 21st

You see darkly through a glass, says the Father. I am going to help you. I am going to grind you new lenses by which to see and perceive My Kingdom and the world around you. I am going to bring fresh clarity and precision to what you see and how you perceive things in the spiritual realm.

As you see new and different things, realize that this is not truly new or different. You have been trafficking in this realm your whole life, and you just did not realize it. The Kingdom of God is your native habitat.

Yes, there are other things that will try to get your attention like spoiled and disobedient children. Do not mind them or encourage them by giving them heed. The enemy always wants your thoughts on what he is doing and what he is planning. Just sweep his strategies aside by your faith-filled prayers as I show them to you, and keep your eyes fixed on Me.

You will have visitations, says the Father, for now is that time in your life. I am bringing the visitations of glory to cleanse and to recalibrate your spirit from the demands of natural things and the distraction of earthly matters. I am attuning you like never before in your life to commiserate and access the heavens that you might participate with Me in the work I am doing now.

July 22nd

My faithfulness in your life is activated by corresponding actions on your part, says the Father. The Kingdom of God is not accessed by passive observation. Your download from the glory is activated on a day-to-day basis as you participate with Me moment by moment.

Even as you rise this day, open your heart and your ears to My voice. My voice brings My Kingdom, and My voice is My rule in your life. Look into your intuitive sense for it is designed to reflect and reveal My instructions to you by a continual flow of communication through the Holy Spirit.

Feed yourself on My Word. Out of My Word I will impart strength to you and affirm that I am with you, making Myself known and auditing every second of your life. Respond to the tug of the Holy Spirit on you to do and say what I inspire you to do and say. Refuse to be drawn away or distracted by outside influences, temptations, or distractions. In so doing you will be an obedient child, reflecting who I am in the earth. The enemy will see this and be blinded by who I am. He will not be able to look past who I am in you to launch an attack against your natural man (who you are in your human vulnerability). This is how I clothe you with Myself. Be thus clothed with Myself today, and walk in the grace and victory which you have been asking of Me.

July 23rd

I am not a forgetful God, says the Father. I would also ask that you not forget: do not forget your dreams, your aspirations, or those things that I promised and that you believed. It has been a long time coming, but I am the God that inhabits eternity. Therefore, because I have time, you have time.

Abraham believed past the time it made sense to believe. He maintained hope even when all hope was lost. He held his hopes in his arms and dandled his hopes on his knees, and he laughed! That is why he named his son "Isaac" (laughter). Do not allow the sorrows and disappointments of the past take the laugh of faith from your lips. Look upon the sarcasm of the unbelievers and even the dry bones of your own destitute expectations and say, "Ah ha! Bah, ha, ha!"

You shall yet know the substance of those things for which you are hoping. I say to you, recapture your dreams. Resurrect the slumbering hopes that I planted in you so long ago, and dare to believe that your Father can and will do anything and move any obstacle to bring those hopes into a reality in your life this day, says the Father.

July 24th

Say within yourself today and every day, "'He came that I might have life and have life more abundantly." Abundance is your natural state. As you cultivate an "abundance" mentality, what I have done for you on Calvary will begin to permeate and saturate the most-hardened strata of unbelief and religious thinking in your makeup. I will break up the bedrock of religious death and cause new life to spring up and bear fruit in answered prayers.

Let those unthinkable prayers be lifted to My throne today, says the Father. I stand at the ready to receive and answer the audacious and faith-filled prayers.

July 25th

My voice is My Kingdom, says the Father. Your participation in response to My voice is your participation with My Kingdom. It is through much tribulation that you enter into the Kingdom constituted by My voice. That tribulation (that manifold pressure) is comprised of all the other voices demanding your attention.

You are where your attention takes you. If you give heed to the voice of circumstance, the voice of the dark one, or the voices of those around you who are reacting to what they see in you and about you, you will be distracted from My voice.

Determine today that you will be a child of the "one voice"—My voice that is guiding you and positioning you in the center of My peace, My righteousness, and My joy. In so doing you will not only deliver yourself from the snares of the enemy but will receive that deliverance you have been crying out for My hand to bring in your life.

July 26th

Daily bread is best made fresh. Would you not agree? Rejoice, says the Father, when I serve it up warm and wonderful every morning instead of two days before you actually need it. There is no shortage of provision in My Kingdom, says the Father. I am not shrewdly withholding that which you have asked me for as though I had some inscrutable reason to keep you in lack.

Draw on My provision, says the Father. Call for it even as I called for the fig tree to dry up from the roots because it had no figs in the time of ripe fruit. I am the provisioning God, and I would like you to participate with Me in the miraculous provisioning that is on inventory in the glories for you today.

Draw on My provision by your faith-filled prayers. Let your petitions be pregnant with expectation! The birthing of your blessing time is at hand.

July 27th

Let My peace rule in your heart, says the Father. Refuse to worry about anything! I have given you all things that are necessary for life and for walking in communion and cooperation with My Kingdom. Yes, there are challenges. There are giants in your land and on the horizon. If they could devour you, they would have already.

The enemy is not after you, says the Father, He is actually after the God in you. The only way he can come at Me is by coming at Me in you. I will not tolerate this, and I will not allow the enemy to harass you because of who I am on the inside of you. I am rising up in you today to roll back the heavy burdens. Be lightened, says the Father. My yoke is easy. My burden is light. Say within yourself every day, "Yoke easy, burden light."

Reject every inward thing that is contrary to My promise. This is the day of lightening and joy and the exuberant acknowledgement of My watch-care over even minute issues in your life, says the Father.

July 28th

When I look at you, says the Father, I do not see failure. When I look at you, I see Myself reflected in your heart. When I move in your life, I am acting to cooperate with Myself in My own sovereign purposes. The whole point of the Cross was to take away every disqualification that might give Me pause from acting in your life.

As you pray to Me and commune with Me, I find no impediment to our intimacy. Drink deeply of My Spirit today, says the Father, for I am drinking deeply of your humanity. I will not be denied in My passion for you, and I will not deny you.

I am not reluctant to answer your heart's cry. I am not hesitant to act in your behalf. Call out to Me; ask, seek, knock. In the asking you will be rewarded, in the seeking you will discover, and in the knocking there will be opened to you a door that no man can shut.

July 29th

I am writing Myself into your life today, says the Father. I am interrupting the litany of failure and frustration and bringing to your day the narrative of My Spirit. It is a new day. The fresh wind of My Spirit is blowing away the ashes of past disappointments.

- For bitterness, I will give sweetness.
- For sorrow and heaviness I am now giving you lightness and joy.
- For deprivation and loss I am substituting provision and restoration.

I am giving back to you what time, happenstance, and life itself have deprived you. There is nothing lost that I cannot and will not restore in your life.

Put your trust in Me. My recovery program in your life starts today. You will walk in the garden of My blessing and know the fullness of what the gift of Christ has purchased on your behalf.

July 30th

I am pouring out the breaker-anointing oil, says the Father. The things that have blocked and impeded your answers will hold you no longer. As your worship reaches the throne, so My delivering hand reaches you in your circumstance. I am crushing the forces in opposition against you.

My horn is exalted in your midst, says the Father. The covenant of salvation, preservation, and deliverance has been ratified, and the resources of heaven's inventory are now released over your head. The heavens that once were brass are now opened, and your answers wait for the occasion of your faith-filled prayers.

It is a new day, says the Father, with a new beginning and a new ending. I am rewriting your destiny. The dark one and his strategies are being foiled, and your victory is assured. Rejoice this day in that expectation, and claim this victory as your own.

July 31st

There is Holy anger in My character, says the Father. It smolders white hot at the oppressor and the accuser. I am come now, even today, to put to flight the enemy of your soul who dared to touch the apple of My eye.

I will move off far from you those who have misrepresented Me and those who have persecuted you. They claimed the authority of My name, but it is My name that shall occupy them elsewhere while you go free as a bird from the hand of the fowler.

You will not be a prey in the hands of your enemies, says the Father. They will not succeed against you for I have written the record of your tomorrows that you shall go free!

August 1st

You are a principality, says the Father. You are seated with Christ in the highest (far above all those dominions and powers who have acted to usurp My plans in the earth). I am activating in you this day the righteousness of Christ, and everything you say and do will be as effective as if I said it and did it.

Choose your words wisely, says the Father, for they will be the harbingers of My power in the earth. Tear down the strongholds, and bind the strong man. Declare your city to be free from the workings of the evil one. This day I give you authority to rend the predator and to rescue even your loved ones and your little ones from the maw of the predator who thought he had completely escaped.

I will deliver your little ones into your hands, and salvation will come to your whole house. I will not fail to answer your heart's cry. Let this decree rest upon your lips and rise in your throat as a cry of liberty.

August 2nd

My government and My peace are increasing in your life, says the Father. My dominion is expanding into new territory in your life, and today you will begin to experience afresh and anew the difference the Cross makes in the blood-bought life of a believer.

My peace is not born of compromise but of total and complete annihilation of the adversary. No more crying in the night, says the Father. No more sleepless seasons of worry and fear. My peace I leave with you. From this day forward your sleep shall be sweet and your composure shall be fortified by My grace and My power.

I am renewing your youth that I might implement the promised blessing of years before this present time. You believed Me, and you trusted Me. This day I make good upon that confidence you placed in Me for you will not be ashamed and you will not be disappointed any longer.   Those that laughed and even mocked you to your face will see My hand and know that you are the chosen recipient of My particular blessing and favor.

August 3rd

Cast your care upon Me today, says the Father. Be assured that there is no problem so large nor any need so minute that I would choose to leave you without My kind assistance. I sent My Son to address your greatest need, and with equal abandon I have made all the resources of glory available to you for every other challenge.

Be provisioned with those things which are needed. Receive of My peace. I am calming the storm that is out of your natural ability to quell. I am giving you favor where favor is needed. I am sending healing grace to touch that area of your body where there is a need. I am touched with every area of your need, and I am responding as one who cares deeply and is able to make the difference.

Receive My watchful, meticulous care over your life today for this is the day that all sense of being neglected by Divine Providence is eradicated from your life.

August 4th

I am the Rock of Ages, says the Father. I am about to rock your world and the world of those around you. I am going to begin with pebbles, and before I am through I am going to work up to boulders, says the Father.

I am going to rain hailstones of truth down on the strongholds of the enemy, and his battlements will be crushed and ruined in your life. Receive My truth in your life, says the Father.

- The truth of your position in Me.
- The truth of your deliverance.
- The truth of your provision.
- The truth of your healing and your restoration.

Enter into My timelessness and My irreducible life, says the Father. Enter into the armory of My glory, and arm yourself for the taking of the spoil for I have assured the outcome of the battle that you face today.

August 5th

No more delays, says the Father. Hope deferred makes the heart sick, but I am the Tree of Life that is available now to answer every heart's cry. Your blessing time has come. You have sown and sown, and I have seen every seed that you have planted. This day I am giving you assurance of your recompense. Do not forget about your plantings, says the Father, for I have not forgotten. Out of the good ground of your heart, I will cause the yield of blessing to come forth in the appointed time.

Now is that time; no more delays! Look into your heart. Look into the mirror that I am on the inside of you, and say boldly, "No more delays!" Surely this is not just the day, but this is the hour of My faithfulness, and I will give you the receipt of the substance of your faith.

August 6th

Take no thought for the morrow, says the Father, for I have endowed you today to overcome the threats that tomorrow holds. There is no obstacle, no barrier, and no impediment in your way that will not yield to the authority I have laid upon your shoulders. Clothe yourself with who I am in the situation, and be shed of the garments of weakness, vulnerability, and frailty. There is no frailty in Me, says the Father. Consequently, there is vitality and strength in you.

All power is given to Me in heaven and in earth, and I am activating that fact in your life today. Let your declaration be bold against the enemies of lack, sorrow, and death. Open your mouth and boldly declare:

No more!
Never again!
This far and no further!

This day I will make good on every promise I have made, so be very bold and very courageous, says the Father.

August 7th

The Father says, I am sending the wind of My remembrance upon you this day. The floods of adversity and destruction are abating, and there is a new potential in evidence over every aspect of your life.

My wind is passing over your life for I have remembered you. You prayed, you waited, and you wondered if things would ever change. Change is upon you, and it is wrought by My hands. There were those who claimed you were suffering because it was My will and My determinate purpose. They did not speak for Me, and their words were corrupted by religious contamination.

My words over you are life-giving because they proceed from My heart. My words alight upon you and breathe life within and around you. With that life comes fruitfulness, abundance, and provisioning. Expect it. Expect to see it in the most devastated part of your life today.

August 8th

You have asked Me to take you to the next level in the prophetic, says the Father, and I have determined to respond to that request. Therefore, I am not simply going to change what you hear; I am going to change how you hear.

You are going to discern My voice with greater frequency and clarity. You are going to open your eyes in the morning, and you will hear My words before you hear your own thoughts. Your dreams will no longer merely arise from the random residue of the day's business, but more and more they will constitute experiences of visitation from Me.

You will begin to sort through things you have heard in yourself and from others, and you will discard things and words that were unclear for I am going to bring My thoughts, words, and visions into crystal clarity in your spirit. You will know what it means to say, "Whether in the body or out of the body, I know not."

Prepare yourself because with greater clarity of spirit comes greater accountability and responsibility to act upon what I tell you. I am compressing time and bringing a greater intensity of anointing into your life. Receive it as from Me, says the Father, for it is in answer to the very prayers you have unwittingly prayed.

August 9th

I have imparted to you my irreducible life, says the Father. Who I am cannot be diminished in you. Who I am cannot be taxed or drained or emptied in any way. I am the high and lofty one who inhabits eternity, and I bring that environment wherever I am. Because I live in you, I have, therefore, placed eternity in your heart.

In your heart is a timeless, boundless, fullness of life on the inside of you that cannot be assaulted by any enemy. As you pray and as you petition Me daily, the door opened within you is opened, and the eternity inside you that surrounds Me flows out into your life as answered prayer. I have made this available as a stipend of a heavenly account at your disposal for every need.

Use what I have accorded you, says the Father, and trust in My supply. You have lived far below your privileges, but we are about to rectify that in every area of life. Are you ready? Trust Me, says the Father. Things are about to get better.

August 10th

The incorruptible seed by which you were born again, says the Father, is not a seed any longer. Once conceived in your heart, it grew into a child and from a child into the one new man that is the new creation.

Old things are passed away, says the Father. I have removed your past as far from Myself as east is from west. If I am not mindful of things gone by, why would you be? Do not allow your past to dictate your future. Your future is not controlled by your past, or your disability, or what people think or say. Who are they anyway? Yes, My words in the heavens eclipse every word spoken contrary to who I say you are since they tried to sell you that bill of goods. They were sunk by the same accusation they tried to torpedo on you.

You are the redeemed! You are the ransomed! You are that one who has received the entitlement from My throne. Now be seated, says the Father. Be seated far above all principality and power, and make My enemies your footstool by the words of your mouth. If you say it, I will do it, says the Father. If you will not say it, I will not do it.

August 11th

Strike while the iron is hot, says the Father. When My Spirit comes upon you in waves of overpowering joy, you are at that moment standing in My Kingdom. My Kingdom is righteousness, joy, and peace.

When My joy and My peace come upon you, that is the time (the very second) to decree your decrees and make your words known in the heavens. For in that moment everything you say and do will be as effective as if I said it or did it. Have I not said in My Word that with joy you shall draw water out of the well of salvation? When the joy comes upon you (supernatural, overwhelming joy), draw from the waters of salvation at that moment and pour them out by your declarations upon your dry and thirsty land.

Your answers and your heart's desires will spring forth like tender plants and grow to be mighty oaks, bearing forth your blessing and blessings to others. This is the working of My Kingdom in you and through you.

My joy will come. It will bubble in you and become effervescent in the depths of your being. It will burst forth out of you in waves of euphoria, and those around you will look and question, "What is wrong with you?" You will be unable to answer for the rivers of joy will be flooding out of you like a mighty river.

There is healing in that river. There is deliverance. There is every answer to every desire. The river of joy is the river that carries your destiny and your heart's desire from the inventories of the glory into your life as a manifest declaration and substantial hope. It is yours, says the Father. Yield to it, cooperate with it, allow it to come, and be bold to declare it as it manifests in your life.

August 12th

I am restricting your fidelity to Me alone, says the Father, for I have focused the full faithfulness of My right arm on you and your destiny. I have no other agenda than to bless you, accelerate your destiny, and set you in the fullness of My plans for your life. Even as I told Abram to get out away from that which was familiar, I will not allow any place, person, or purpose to lay claim on you other than Myself.

I am opening the inventories of the glory and placing them at your disposal. There will be many who will come and ask you to be a source of prosperity for them. I say to you, "Only do what you see the Father do."

Get ready! Get ready! Get ready, says the Father. It is a new day and a new responsibility. Your life will no longer be defined by what you lack but by what I have provisioned you with beginning today.

August 13th

I have given you a name, says the Father. I have ordained that name to be your defense in time of trouble and your shelter in a time of storm. Breathe that name in this night, and the angels will hasten to your cause and personally attend to the very beating of your heart. I brought that name into the garden as My children were vainly knitting leaves to hide their shame. They did not understand My name because their minds were darkened. Yet, I have enlightened your mind. Blessed be your mind for it perceives and understands the strength of My name and the cost to place it at your disposal.

Breathe My name, says the Father. Breathe it in, and breathe it out. Let My name be the wind that drives your enemy as though with a tempest far from you. Let My name be the gentle breeze in the night that comforts you with the assurance, "Fear not, it is I."

August 14th

I am going to begin to speak to you in your common everyday vernacular, says the Father. My words will no longer be veiled or obtuse in any way. I will speak to you on your level because you have made a decision to listen to Me on My level.

My sound is not as the sound of men. Since man fell I have been whirling in the breezes of the day, sending forth My sound. Enoch heard that sound, and he echoed that sound back to Me. Do you want to walk with Me as he did and experience what he experienced? There is more than that in store for you.

Men and their institutions have presumptuously concluded that they understand and can frame My works and what the future holds. Man's future never arrives, but My future is always now. Walk in My now, and you will find Me. I will be found of you, and I will place My whirlwinds on the inside of you that they might flow out and establish My will, My purpose, and My environment of dominion in all that you undertake, represent, and purpose to do.

August 15th

There is no flight response in My Spirit, says the Father, and I am removing such from the inside of you. You will run to the battle. You will be of good courage and fight the good fight. I will curse him that

135

curses you, and I will execrate him that trifles with you.

Go ahead and exhibit divine insolence in the face of the enemy. You will not turn your back on the opposition, says the Father. I am with you, and you will win the day against your adversary. Do not be dismayed at their looks. Do not be terrorized by the terror they would use to terrify you. You will not flee from your enemy. Your enemy will flee from you in mindless confusion because I am with you.

August 16th

There is a tsunami of My Spirit abreast in your life, says the Father. There is an inbound wave of My Spirit provoked by a disturbance in My Kingdom against the enemy of your soul. Find your high ground in Me for I am shaking all the illegitimate authority (all that can be shaken) so that only My righteousness, peace, and joy will remain and abide over your life.

The enemy thought he would bind you. The enemy thought he would impede you. The enemy of your soul dared to draft a strategy against you and against what the blood of My Son paid for in your life.

I will not tolerate the enemy that would dare trifle with you, My child, let alone actually presume to do you harm. I know that is not what you have been taught by some who thought they had to defend My seeming inaction at times. There have been those misguided servants who thought to explain away suffering and the severity of life as though some mystical purpose was served by your pain.

What suffering do you now endure that the Cross did not pay for you? What deprivation that the emptying of Myself on the Cross did not fill? I place no premium on your suffering, My child. You have heard this before, and you have hoped that it was true. Look over your shoulder. I am sweeping away the opposition. I am bringing healing, restoration, deliverance, and provision today. This is that day to which you cried out, so let your trust be in My hand. I will never leave you, and I will never forsake you. Things are about to get better, says the Father. Do not you agree it is about time?

August 17th

The Father says today that never again will insecurity rule you. Never again will your past define you. Today you step out of time and into eternity. From this day forward you are timeless and limitless and bounded only by My love for you and your faith in that love in who I am.

Today I pour Myself into your now and draw you into Myself. No longer are you an earth-dweller for today I activate your seat with Me in heavenly places. You are a principality. You are a power. All power is given to Me, and all power I bequeath to you from the foot of the Cross.

Articulate your faith, says the Father. From this day forward let your prayers be verbally articulate in the heavens. They will arise before Me attended by the angels that have been assigned to you from before your conception. Your prayers arise as a sweet-smelling savor that provokes the might of My arm and the power of My hand in your life.

Open your mouth wide, and I will fill it. Broaden your faith, and I will cause your faith to become substance upon the earth in your life. I give you an open heaven, so walk under it as one entitled to what the Cross affords. I break up the fountains of the deep and open the four rivers of Eden in the depths of your soul. You are impregnable within Me from this day forward.

August 18th

Relinquish the outcome, says the Father, for the seed must fall into the ground and come to germination before it will produce the desired end. That thing you have believed Me for, asked Me for, petitioned Me for you do not have to keep asking Me about because I have answered.

I have answered you in the form of a seed. I have ratified your request and written the requisition on heaven's inventory. Yet, there is one more thing for you to do. Release the vision to Me. Relinquish the vision that I might breathe on it and cause it to come to fruition in due time.

You ask, "Haven't I done this? Haven't I let go and trusted you?" The Father answers that you will know you have relinquished the outcome when you leave the details to Me and stop trying to tell Me how to answer. You are supposed to ask what ye will, but the details are My purview, says the Father. You create an unnecessary delay as long as you keep telling Me how to answer.

When is the due time? It is in the now that you will enter when you relinquish the outcome. Plant the seed, and go away and sleep night and day. I am the responsible party that will cause the things you believe Me for to come up, produce, and be fashioned. I want this as much as you do, says the Father.

August 19th

Relieve yourself from the burden of busyness, says the Father. The enemy has snared you with the urgent so that he might rob you of the important. There is one thing that is necessary; that is, to sit at My feet and learn of Me.

You can hurl yourself at the day with ferocity and effort, says the Father, or you can become truly effective and relinquish the burdens of the day to Me. Do you honestly think I have destined you for this rat race? Calm yourself like a child suckled at the breast of his mother. Still your mind before Me this morning; then, move forward in the stillness. I will show you the quantum leap over the unproductive, demanding activities of the day and bring you to true fruitfulness.

You know exactly why you received this today.

August 20th

You did not think you would get this far, says the Father, did you? What makes you think I cannot take you the rest of the way? You feared your enemies would discover that you were a fraud and could not possibly pull off what you are trying to convince others you can do.

It was all bravado and false courage--or was it? Perhaps it was rather the Christ in you standing up and drawing the sword of Himself from the scabbard of your inner man and simply believing that all things are possible.

Do not quit now, says the Father. You have just now got their attention. Go show them what I am really capable of in you.

August 21st

Look for My fingerprints in your day. I have gone out before you while you slept and placed My fingerprints on the subconscious minds of those you will encounter today. You will have several divine encounters, and you will know them by the stillness that will assert itself when you look into peoples' eyes. When you see Me in their faces, speak to Me in them, and I will answer you. They will then be brought closer to My Kingdom.

Proclaiming the gospel is not about quotations and memorization. It is about knowing Me when you see Me and allowing Me to bridge the gap and make the connection between you and the hurting and lost. In this way you do not just talk about Me--you demonstrate Me and bring salvation to those in need.

August 22nd

What are you waiting for, asks the Father? What condition has to be met before you vault over the rail and walk on water? I say to you that Calvary met every condition for water-walking faith. The furnace you are in right now would have consumed you but for the miracle of My preserving power in the midst of the mess you are in.

You have cried out for miracles and the miraculous, and I say to you it is a miracle that you are still here. The enemy, left unfettered, would have taken you out long ago. If I retrained him from a thousand efforts to do you harm, why would you give heed to the present threat or future intimidations of this toothless tiger? Yes, he roars, but only the old lion roars because he is no longer able to snare the prey. So when you "run to the roar," says the Father, you know that is one direction in which you will encounter no harm. Yes, there are hidden snares and lurking enemies, but I have taken them into account. Did I not tell you I would protect you from the words whispered against you in secret counsels and private quarters?

The false prophets peep and mutter to the false brethren because they know their days are numbered and their words are impotent to ensnare My sons and My daughters. You are mine, says the Father. I will not allow any man or woman to set on thee to hurt or harm you in any way. So, go ahead and venture out. Do not say, "There is a lion in the street!" for the lion in the street will become the trophy on your mantle if you will but venture forth in my name and my boldness to seize the victory I have already afforded you.

August 23rd

I have felled the "tree of the knowledge of good and evil," says the Father. I severed its corrupt root and destroyed its contaminated fruit 2000 years ago by the act of the Son on Calvary. I said in My immutable counsel, "Why encumber the ground?"

Why then would you choose the rotting bread-fruit of this twice-dead monstrosity over the verdant leaves and succulent fruit of the "Tree of Life?" I am the tree of life, says the Father, and the leaves of My limbs are for the healing of the nations. I have bent My boughs low so that even My little ones might reach them and partake and be satisfied.

The natural mind refuses to live by the words of My mouth, says the Father. The natural mind wants to weigh things out, judge circumstances, situations, and people and then make its decisions. How is that working for you? Come unto Me, and I will satisfy your life with the "words of life" from the limbs of the Cross. I will gather up that carcass of dead hopes and dreams into My arms. Look your destiny in the face, and say "live!"

Are you ready? You know exactly why you received this prophesy today.

August 24th

Come unto Me all who are burdened and heavy laden, and I will give you rest. Why are you straining and struggling, says the Father? Even your body is showing the wear and stress of the cares that are on your shoulders. Cast all your cares on Me! Saddle Me with all the weight and heaviness, and I will bear them hence from your life and your experience into the wilderness of "never to trouble you anymore."

There is no agenda, no plan, no purpose in My choices for you that validate or justify the brutal struggles you have borne up under. I break off illegitimate authority over you today, says the Father. Take a deep breath, and let all burdens go. I give you sweet sleep from this day forward. I am sending the angels to attend to your slumber. You will commune with the King in the night seasons and walk in the Kingdom in the day.

This day is the line of demarcation, says the Father. Today everything changes. The chains fall off and will never to be borne by you again.

August 25th

I am lifting you up into My love, says the Father. Today, you begin afresh and anew your ascent into Me for love is who I am. I will never leave you. I will never forsake you. I will never cease to be the "yoke easy, burden light." I will never cease to be the light to your path. I will never cease to be the enlargement to your steps.

I am the causation and substance of blessing that is flowing to every area of need in your life. You have asked, "Father, what is your will for my life?" My reply, says the Father, is what do you need? What do you need Me to be in your life today? Articulate that need, declare that need, and I will be made manifest in every void, every ache, and every need in your life. I am your answer, and I am your life and breath even this day.

August 26th

I am the God of the heavens, says the Father. I am the God of the heavens where I have prepared a place for you to sit with Me. At the blast of My nostrils, the mountains lifted their crags toward the sky. At My glance the highest peaks bowed down upon the plains in fear of My might. It is My Spirit of might that is upon you today.

I have not called you to humble yourself to flesh. I have called you to humble yourself to Me while I make all flesh your footstool. Did you think I would leave you powerless to free yourself from the illegitimate authority that plagues you? I am your God and your Father. I will not tolerate any situation, influence, or person to impede, persecute, or harm you in any way.

Lift your hopes up to Me today, and go forth in the audacity of the sonship that the blood of My Son has afforded you. Be bold, says the Father, for you do know Me. I will be known of you, and I will cause all about you to know that you are My beloved and that he that touches you touches the pupil of My eye.

August 27th

The Father says that there is no longer time in your life for lingering doubts or venal pursuits. What price do you place on your integrity? I have provided a path of progress away from the failure and heartbreak of the past. It is up to you to leave behind the patterns of behavior through which you contributed to those past disappointments and defeats.

Receive My enabling grace. Receive the grace that came upon Saul of old when he was changed into another man when My Spirit came upon him. Open your mouth, and let My words enter into the deepest part of your being even as they flow out to establish My dominion over all the works of the enemy in your situation.

Allow My character to flow in and My authority to flow out of your heart and your mouth today, says the Father. This is the respiration of My Spirit in the lives of those who choose to live yielded to Me.

Without this respiration of spirit, you die away from your connection with Me. You are not destined to be a dry tree without fruit. You are full of the sap of My substance. Allow this sap to permeate every aspect of your life, and you will indeed bear much fruit unto Me and on your own behalf.

August 28th

It is not polite to finish someone's sentences, says the Father. I am the first and the last in all things pertaining to your life. When you look at the situation, it may seem that all is not well, but I have the final say. Your past does not dictate your future; your present is not dependent on your past.

Who told you that you were naked? Who told you that you had to solve the problem? Who said that you were to blame? There have been those who have blamed you, says the Father, but even though they quoted Scripture, they did not speak My mind.

I have said that you are the righteousness of Christ. I have said you can do all things through Christ. I have said I am the God who is more than enough. Let your words come into agreement with Me and not with what the circumstance, situation, or other people are declaring things about you.

You are not a failure.
You are not at fault.
You are not to blame.

You are My son, My daughter. Let your trust forever be in Me for I am the One who brings the dawn of blessing anew over every morning. It is going to be a great day, says the Father. Get out and enjoy it to the full.

August 29th

I came that you might have life and have it more abundantly, says the Father. How does an earthquake or a hurricane fit into that plan? Yet man (in his foolishness) calls these things "an act of God." This is a contradiction to my character, and this manner of thinking impugns the work of the Cross.

I came that you might have an irreducible life that puts you over the top in every avenue of human endeavor. I created man for dominion. I created you for dominion. I placed it in your DNA to subdue and rule your environment. I take no pleasure in suffering. I place no premium on pain, loss, or any harm that might come to you or any other person.

When I look into your heart, I do not see an offender that needs to be punished. I see the Lamb that was slain from the foundation of the world. To judge you or harm you or bring calamity, sickness, or poverty upon you would be tantamount to crucifying My Son again by My own hand.

Welcome to the new reality, says the Father. The reality of a son or of a daughter beloved in My eye, endeared in My heart, and protected by My hand.

August 30th

Today, says the Father, you now possess the gates of your enemies--not because of who you are or what you have done but because of who I am in you and what I did for you 2000 years ago. The efficacy of the work of the cross is bringing My blessing and protection to you even this day. The enemy can no longer lay an ambush against you. He cannot even go out or come in without authorization from you.

This day you are a principality. Satan is fallen as lighting from heaven. You are seated with Me in the heavens, and Satan is unseated from his place of usurpation over your life. All eyes are upon you, and all ears are attuned to your words. Open your mouth, and pray with entreaty. Declare with authority, and decree with finality. My breath is in your words.

You know exactly why you received this word today.

August 31st

You are not only dealing with crooked people, says the Father, but you are dealing with crooked places. The steps of your feet have led you into a place where everyone has an angle, and there are many agendas (hidden and otherwise). Fret not, says the Father, for I am with you and have sent the straightening angel from My presence. The crooked places will be made straight. The hidden agendas will be exposed. The twisted plans of crooked people will be rendered inert, and you will be the one left standing when the dust settles.

There are gates of judgment and bars of oppression that have been raised to hem you in and keep you out, says the Father, but I will melt the gates of brass and the iron bars with the blast of My nostrils. You will sit in the gates and rule with the words of your mouth and the prayers of your lips.

Let your mouth pray. Let your words be heard. I will be petitioned by you and will hear the cry of your heart and answer speedily by My might.

September 1st

There can be no compromise with the enemy, says the Father. He has stolen from you, therefore, he must restore seven-fold that which you were robbed. He mocked you, therefore, he will be humbled at your feet. I decree to you this day that you will bring back (not just some, not just a portion) all the goods, all the people, and all the things that have been stolen from you.

I am doing a restorative work in your life. From your perspective all My paths are peace. From the enemy's perspective it is all-out war. I will stop at nothing less than slaughter. I will not yield or accept any partial deliverance. I decree to you this day that you will recover the spoils--all the spoil. You will overcome until there is no more to overcome.

You are My beloved, says the Father, and I am pleased to do this work in your life, in your situation, and in your circumstance.

Number the days, mark the time, and know that even today it begins!

September 2nd

I have established My paternity in you, says the Father. The very DNA of My nature is molding you and shaping you. It is your nature to trend upward and not down. The stain of sin is expunged. The taint of the fall and the residue of the curse have no root in you. Now, walk out of the house of bondage, be shed of the grave clothes of mourning, and relinquish the grasping mentality of poverty, want, and lack for I am provisioning you this day.

I am protecting you. I am assigning you your portion with the mighty as you stand up and decree, declare, and proclaim who I am in your life. Do not acknowledge what the enemy is threatening to do, but instead, acknowledge what I am doing and have done for you.

I laugh and mock at the enemy of your soul. I see you as a child boldly standing between the knees of his Father, taunting the enemy, and then looking up at the approval on My face. I see you mock the enemy, and My heart leaps as I say, "YES," says the Father, for I have poured My Kingdom, My government, and My dominion within you to produce an heir that will subdue the earth and make known My glories in your life and the lives of the captives around you.

September 3rd
The Father says today that the blessings of Abraham are apportioned you through the Cross. Even as I promised Abraham, so I entitle you. The blessings of Abraham are the dividends of the work of Calvary on your behalf. The blessings of Abraham accrue to you through the blood of the Son.

I will make you a great nation. You are a holy nation, a royal priesthood. I say over you, "Thy kingdom come." You are a kingdom of priests and prophets unto My name. I say over you, "I will make your name great." I have adopted you into the God kind of life. You bear My name, and My name will be great in you and great through you in the earth and in your generation (even this generation), says the Father.

146

I will bless you. I will bring you to your knees in gratitude for the overwhelming miraculous work that I am doing in your earth this day. You shall be a blessing. All those who come into proximity to your life will be blessed. The people around you and those who favor you and deal honestly and favorably with you will not fail to notice the overwhelming blessing that comes upon them when they so entreat you. The men and women of the earth will lay awake nights seeking creative ways to bless you because they know the benefits of blessing you. They will become beneficiaries of your blessings when they attach themselves to you for good.

I will curse him that curses you. I will not tolerate him that trifles with you. My hand will deal abruptly with those that seek to harm you and defame you unjustly. The earth shall tremble under them, and they will not be able to find safety or security in the earth because they have chosen to set themselves up as judges concerning you. That I shall not tolerate. I will not endure the man or the woman that acts contrary to what the Cross paid for in your life.

In you all the families of the earth will be blessed--families of men and families of businesses. In you I will set the solitary in families and restore the table of fellowship that has been neglected among men. Let hand strike with hand, says the Father. I will breathe the breath of My blessing upon those that choose to agree with My promise and walk in agreement with one another.

This is your portion. I would that you lay claim on it and say, "This is mine, and this is for me." In doing so you activate and open heaven, bringing a new season in your life today, says the Father.

September 4th

My family is not an institution, says the Father. The love in My heart for you does not require pulpits, pews, or denominational structure to find its expression in your heart and life. I am moving into your life in a new and fresh way. I will not be bound by the things man defines as My place in the earth.

My love for you defies definition. My intense care for you exceeds all boundaries. As the passions of the Cross were upon Me, I was not picturing steeples and church buildings. I was picturing your face, your heart, your life, and the difference the shedding of My blood would make in you, through you, and for you.

Lay claim to your place in My family. Wrap yourself protectively in the passion of My love for you. Know that I do not see you as merely a supportive contributor to the culture of Western Christianity. You are not a cog in the religious machine. When I see you, I see the prospect of intimate communion with you as the prize for which I groaned and for which I cried out in triumph at My last human heartbeat--"It is finished."

In these days I am disassembling the constituent cultural components that have extended the tentacles of religious death toward My Kingdom. They will die and fall away, and My children will come awake and find themselves sitting at the table of their Father. The meal is prepared, the angelic servers are ready, and the earth is groaning for My sons and My daughters to take their place in the Father's family. This is the ache of My heart and the travail of My soul, and it shall be satisfied.

September 5th

Leave the details to Me, says the Father. There is much effort wasted in prayer when people try to tell Me how to go about answering their need. Then when I do not act according to their instructions, they (wrongly) conclude I do not want them to have the thing they requested.

I will take care of the details, says the Father. Simply pray the things you desire, and leave the details to Me. I will go about arranging your life, moving behind the scenes, and preparing the answer according to My sovereign processes. Trying to tell Me how to go about bringing the answer is a sign of unbelief. If you will relinquish the outcome to Me, you will look back on the end of the matter and, giving thanks, declare of Me, "You do all things well!"

Bring your petition this day, and do not pray a modified prayer for less than you desire. That is not humility; that is manipulation. Do not tell Me how to answer or dictate the terms and conditions regarding how you expect Me to act. Simply ask! Ask that your joy may be full. Your asking is the preamble to My answering. I am the God who answers, says the Father. You are going to have to ask Me.

September 6th

The Father says today that love never stops loving. Love is the one indomitable power in the earth. If love never fails, says the Father, when is it appropriate to turn away from love and treat one another outside of its parameters? Love is the only way to ascend above the negative aspects of the law of sowing and reaping. Only through love can you avoid the bitter consequences of a sinful past.

Let love lead you to a new beginning. Only love (which you are asking of Me) can usher in the new day. As you love, the bitter harvest of regretful choices will be rendered inert, and a new, fresh grace will then be manifested over your life. Love will cause My blessing upon you even when you have made mistakes and wrong choices.

Do not leave the path of love. Forsake not unconditional love for those who forsake love forsake their own mercy and plunge themselves into many hurtful and unnecessary sufferings.

September 7th

It is a new season, says the Father. Under the old covenant I wrote in stone the incontrovertible maxims of truth. In the new covenant men have thought I would also write in stone, but I do not--I write in sand. People change, things change, and My will for your life changes accordingly. The truth is the unchangeable message. The message remains, but the medium by which I communicate that truth is fluid and changeable.

You are My epistle this day, says the Father. Each day of your life is a page scribed by My hand. Your life is My message to the world of life, hope, joy, and faith. Your life is a tome of hopes realized and dreams fulfilled. I will leave no loose ends, and not one chapter will be seen as a "dark chapter."

I am turning things around. Look for the dawn light beginning to pink up the cast of the morning sky even today. It is a new season. Do not dread, do not fear, and do not despair. I am the difference, says the Father--I am the difference that a day makes!

September 8th

I have called you to be an altar builder, says the Father. Only upon the altar not made with human hands will I receive the life poured out like a drink offering unto Me. There are many things for which men will sacrifice their lives, but only one sacrifice honors Me; that is the sacrifice of service inspired by the work of the Cross. On that ground I will consecrate your seed and the seed after that, and on that ground I will certify the blessing upon your generations.

Every day you arise constitutes an altar upon which you have the opportunity to pour your life out in worship to Me. Worship is more than songs or lifting of hands. Singing and postures of worship do not constitute worship; they merely commemorate the life already poured out to Me. May your life be a drink offering to Me, says the Father.

I will give you water from rock upon which you have poured out your mind, your will, and your emotions in a service of abandonment to My purposes. I will send the miracle of manna upon that ground constituted by your service of worship.

Do you desire to see your family and your loved ones follow after Me? I will give unto your seed the land upon which you make sacrifice to My name. You are the forerunner for your children and your children's children. I swear by My name (for I can swear by no higher) that your seed and your seed's seed will worship Me on the ground consecrated by a poured-out life.

September 9th

Your destiny has brought you to this place, says the Father. There is nothing left to chance in My Kingdom. Chance is a concept symptomatic of man's inability to grasp My sovereignty over every minute aspect of life. Man may toss the coin or pull the voting lever, but the outcome is securely in My grasp.

I have handed down a decision and a destiny in your best interest, says the Father. You are one upon which I have bestowed My favor. My favor is the basis of My provision, My protection, and the activation of My purposes in your life right now. You are not an accident. This day is not some random occurrence on a meaningless time line. Every moment of this day, says the Father, is moving you inexorably toward the total fulfillment of all that the Cross purchased for you.

I would that you prosper and be in good health, says the Father, and I am prospering your soul toward that end. Fear not; be not dismayed or disappointed. There is no setback or possibility of My plan in your life to be derailed. Take your hand off the tiller, and leave the outcome to Me for I am on your side and working on your behalf. Relax! Let Me take it from here.

September 10th

Not everyone will go with you where I am taking you, says the Father. As with Abram, you must let your "lot" go. You know who this is, and you know when the break came. You did not want to face it because you have a heart of love, and you always desire to retain and strengthen relationships.

You know the exact moment when the blessing began to wane. It was not because I was angry or because you stepped out of My will. It was simply time to move on and relinquish those connections that represent the past. In this season you are being launched into your destiny and into your portion in the Kingdom. Everyone cannot go with you, and everyone will not go with you. If you hang on and allow sentimentality to hinder you, there will be unnecessary delays.

Your fidelity belongs to Me, says the Father. I am the friend that sticks closer than any earthly relationship. Give them to Me and move on. I will care for them and yet cause you to be a blessing to them. But, you must draw yourself away with Me. You know exactly who I am talking about, and you know that today is the time and the hour to act.

September 11th

Did you think you would have to wait for eternity before you would rule and reign with Me? The hedge of protection around America changed in 1989, says the Father. This took place when the Berlin Wall came down in Germany and signaled a fundamental shift in the spiritual geography of the earth in modern times.

I heard the cry of My people behind the Iron Curtain, and I brought them freedom and liberty because they humbled themselves and cried out to Me. The principalities that had terrorized the East for a hundred years were unleashed on the West at that time because they did not choose to humble themselves and seek My face. Six years later terrorism came to American soil in Oklahoma City.

Although America and the West may be vulnerable, My hedge of protection yet stands around My people. When Rome fell to the Goths in 475, the Church shined forth as the sun by many acts of miraculous intervention. Even so, I will protect and defend My people in this day, says the Father. I am a wall of fire around you, and you have nothing to fear.

When you see calamity and crisis on the world scene remember, "I am not of this world--I belong to the Living Father who is a wall of fire about Me." Though the enemy counts you as sheep to the slaughter, it does not mean you are sheep to the slaughter. In fact, you are principalities and powers in the earth, and I will move nations and leaders at your words.

The kingdoms of the earth are becoming the kingdoms of God and Christ, says the Father. You are a part of the transition team that will see the culmination of My plans on the earth. Wrap yourself each day in Psalms 91 as a blanket of protection and a cloak of anointing. See through the chaos and the vanities of man, and pray out My mysteries over the earth and even the immediate environment into which you find yourself. I am the King of Kings, says the Father, and I am training you now to rule and reign with Me.

September 12th

     You have had your shoulder to the task for some time, says the Father, and the question has arisen more than once in your heart, "Why?" I have not allowed this season in your life because I take some perverse pleasure in the pressure you are experiencing. There have been those that have charged Me with that motive, but they are mistaken. Just forgive them and their zealous efforts to get you to accept some mystical benefit from the attacks, the pressure, and the battle you have been facing. Forgive them and know you have been in training for reigning with Me.

     The enemy has not yielded to your decision to "suffer in silence" has he? He has not been impressed or backed off at all when you "thanked me" for the trial as your teachers have instructed. It is time to rise up as Samson did from the enticing lap of religious rationalizations for your suffering. It is time to shake the chains of defeated thinking and rend the bonds the zealots of ignorance have wrapped you in with the decrees of your mouth.

     This is not your dwelling place. I have called you to higher things. Come up higher. Look just above you, and you will see My hand extended. Even today, says the Father, I am adding My sinew and My strength to your words and your decrees. I will extend My arm through your words, bring the enemy to his end, and defeat his strategy. It is a new season (a new day), and it is time to serve Me in a new way that leads to the throne, says the Father.

September 13th

     The Father says today that your rewards from My hand do not come in the form or fashion you might think they would come. I do not merely look upon what you have done, but I look upon the heart. You have purposed in your heart to dream a bigger dream, and I am breathing upon that dream. My heart is pleased that you are asking Me for things that are beyond mere human capability. I do not frown on such things, but I reward the largess of heart inside of you that cries out to Me as Jabez did when he said, "Lord, enlarge my coast!"

     You do not have to accomplish a thing, says the Father, before I will reward you as though you had already done it. So, do not be surprised when I come suddenly and sweetly into your life and give a reward for that which you have not even accomplished yet. Just as you accept Me on faith, likewise, I accept you on faith and will extend to you the reward of the dreams and visions you have in your heart.

Do not be surprised that I will not leave you with only a dream or a vision. I am the vision-maker and the one who causes your dreams to be realized. Put your continued confidence in Me, and know that I am pleased by audacious faith. Yes, those around you may think and even say, "Who do you think you are by dreaming such a big dream?" Just smile at them and know when they see that I bring your dream to pass they will be inspired to dream even bigger dreams. The day will come that you will jokingly say to them, "Who do you think you are?" You will rejoice together in My love and My favor that is being activated in you in a greater measure.

September 14th

I would that you have children in My Kingdom, says the Father. My nature is to have a family, and I would extend My family through you and to you. In eternity there will be no pulpits or pews. In eternity there will be no committees or councils or religious synods. In eternity we will enjoy one another as a father and his family. That family begins here and is established now. I am extending and establishing My paternity in you and through you.

You are not merely called to teach, but you are called to nurture those I send to you. Do not hand them off to someone else. You love them. You nurture them. You disciple them into My love, which is the love of a father. There are many teachers, but there are not many kingdom mothers or kingdom fathers. You said, "Lord, I will do anything you ask of Me." I say to you that I am sending you the solitary, the cast-offs, and the orphaned souls that you might be an instrument to bring them into intimacy with Me.

Be a father today, and be a mother today--not just in the natural with your natural children but to the spiritual children I will send your way. Even as I have loved you, extend to them the love from My heart. Love never fails. It will produce in you the things you desire, and it will produce through you the things that I desire. Be an instrument of My love today.

September 15th

The Father says today that you are walking on ground that I have promised to your seed (to the generation after you). You are walking out struggles and overcoming challenges that will make it easier for those who come after you.

You are a pace-setter. You are setting the pace for the next generation. You are making a difference in people's lives that will not be measured in one year or two years but for decades to come. Despair not because of the ongoing resistance. If you were only acting for yourself, you would have arrived at the finish line long ago. But, I trusted you and entrusted you with the privilege of trailblazing the glories for the generation after you.

When the work is culminated, I will tell your story. I will broadcast the story of your exploits in Me to those just coming on the scene, and they will be encouraged. They will say, "If God did that for them, He will surely do it for me!" And yes, I will reproduce your testimony in many lives. Even generations from now there will be many who will carry your spiritual DNA on the inside of them because of the faithfulness you are exhibiting now.

Do not quit; do not throw up your hands; and, do not walk away. You are the overcomer, and you will take the spoil and claim the glory that the Cross has purchased for you.

September 16th

I am sending you into harm's way, but I am your shield and your protection, the Father says today. I will prove My keeping power to many as they witness the lengths I will go to protect, defend, and preserve you in the coming months. Your testimony will be, "I abide in the secret place of the Most High and under the shadow of His wings He does hide me."

I have prepared a table laden with good things for you, says the Father. From its bounty you will find many needful things and many things that I have released to you simply because I love you. I find pleasure in the act of prospering you. Would you not find pleasure in supernaturally providing for those you love? If you (being but dust) would so love and so supply those you love with an imperfect love, just imagine how sweet it is for Me (the God of the universe) to provision you by My hand.

This is a day of proving. You did not ask Me to prove Myself, but I will, nonetheless, prove My faithfulness in you and to you beginning this day in a new and marked way that will be undeniable and sure.

September 17th

The Father says that the enemy is regarding you as a prey. When Abram fled the famine and entered into Egypt, Pharaoh looked upon Abram's wife, Sarai, and took her for plunder. He did not take her because she was displeasing in his eyes but rather because her beauty captivated him and provoked his actions.

The enemy that is assaulting you now is not doing so because you are repugnant to him. Rather, he is attacking because you have the one thing that he does not have--the presence of My Spirit working in and through you. The enemy is not persecuting you because of what you did wrong but because of what you did right. He is not after you. He is after the "God" in you (who I am in you).

I delivered Sarai from Pharaoh when I disclosed who was her true husband. Likewise, in this trial you are facing, I am going to disclose who is your true husband: I am your husband, and you are My bride. This is the hour and the season, says the Father, that My bride truth will be disclosed, and the enemy will be forced to take his hands off of that which is mine.

You are mine, says the Father, and I am yours. Trust Me. Let Me take it from here. I am about to crush the opposition that is moving against you, and you will know victory in this battle.

September 18th

The Father says to keep moving forward. Do not allow the pressures you are under right now give you pause or turn you back. The wilderness is no place to turn to the right or to the left. The battle is no place to look back or to pause and consider your options. The only options before you are surrender to the enemy or to gain victory over him. If you choose to surrender or if you choose to give into the people, the pressure, or predations of the enemy, this will cause you to lose the ground that you have gained.

It may not seem that you are getting ahead. It may not seem that you are walking in victory. I am, however, enlarging your steps before you. I am clearing the obstacles to your destiny and empowering you for a breakthrough. Do not stop or hesitate. Be strong. Be of good courage for I am with you and will never leave you or forsake you.

In this season you are advancing and transitioning to a new day and new place in Me. Do not allow anything, any person, or any pressure cause you to lose out on even one of the rewards that are just ahead.

September 19th

There is a grievous famine in the land, says the Father. It is a famine of hearing the words of the Lord. I would that you prosper and be in health even as your soul prospers. Believe the prophets bring prosperity of soul. The hearing of My Word is the preamble to every level of prosperity.

Is there lack? Is there a deficit that needs to be addressed? He that has ears to hear, let him hear. Start there. Listen to My words and act on them. I will lead you to the still waters and green pastures. My hand is not shortened. The problems at hand are not incapable of being resolved. Simply choose to put your natural mind in check and respond to My voice as it comes from within and without to lead you out of the struggle and into My vast provision.

I have not left you, and I am not being silent. Did I not say that the calamities that befell others will not befall you no matter what the circumstances may be regarding them? You must listen to My voice and act on My Word when it comes to you. I am your breath and your life, and I will not leave you without comfort or leadership. And, you know exactly why you received this today.

September 20th

My Spirit is no longer merely reconnoitering the marketplace, says the Father. It is time for a full-frontal assault to loose the captives and take the spoil. Follow My Spirit, and I will place you in strategic points of attack to bring the victory.

I will give you the tactics to bring down the command structure of the dark one. Principalities and powers will be unseated. The foundations of the prison house will be rocked by the love that never fails. The prison doors will open. Wall Street itself will bend a knee. Multinational corporations will acknowledge what I am doing in the earth.

The business world will pause to catch its breath, seeking to grasp the scope of My Lordship in the mountain of business and finance. The enemy will be taken by surprise and will yield ground he has held for many years. I am a jealous God, says the Father. I am come to claim the investments that I have made in the marketplaces of the earth.

I am come to lay claim to the time, the resources, and the lives laid down on the altar of business. The souls are mine, and the gold is mine. I will etch with the finger of My right hand upon the ramparts of business. My name, Adonai, and the economies of the earth will be reshaped at the breath of My nostrils, says the Father.

September 21st

You do not do everything perfect, says the Father, and I do not care if others think I spoil you. I took that into account when I planned your destiny. Your humanity and your capacity to err do not abrogate My blessing in your life. Those who have suggested that you have to be perfect to be blessed do not take into account the depth of My favor toward you. I am foolishly fond of you. I have even been accused of letting you get away with things that make Me look unfair. I am not concerned about what "they" think about My child-rearing skills. Who are "they" anyway?

I am moving you incrementally each day toward the greater fulfillment of your destiny in Me. You cannot quicken My pace, but you can slow things down unnecessarily. The dark one is constantly bringing distractions your way that are designed to put you in a holding pattern. Avoiding delays is quite simple: keep your eyes upon Me; listen only to My voice; and, come alongside of My plans and respond to them to the best of your ability. In doing so you place yourself in the "sweet spot" of My grace. This is the place where I cause even your mistakes to prosper.

Stop being hard on yourself, and do not blame yourself for failure. You are not a failure; you are a child of God. Your past does not determine your future because you are not a time-bound creature. Listen to My voice and receive My correction. Your character is always undergoing change and transformation to bring you further into My likeness. In the meantime put your foot in the enemy's neck and declare, "Bah ha ha!" You are the victor even in your imperfection.

The Cross has caused you to ascend above the law of sin and death and brought you into the rarified atmosphere of My unmerited favor.

September 22nd

I am bringing you back to a place of new beginnings, says the Father. The territory will look familiar. The exception will be that you are not the same person you were before. You have learned that I am a God of provision. You have learned that I am a God of preservation. You have experienced My protection and will not get fooled again.

Your friends and acquaintances only know who you were before. The changes I have wrought in your inner man will have gone unnoticed. When you walk in a growth pattern with Me, some relationships will go by the wayside and some relationships will be strengthened. Do not spend time grieving over this because change is the inevitable consequence of growth. Hold everything loosely. As you empty your hands and allow Me to reshape your social environment, you will have more time and energy for the Kingdom pursuits I have commissioned for you.

There will be a new connection just ahead. This will be a new friendship that is not based on commonality or compatibility but will be based on My presence and a partnership of service in My Kingdom. You will be seen as an odd couple, and you will be a sign and wonder. Enjoy and embrace this partnership with revelry and abandon. This friendship will be the hallmark of a new transition in your life from where you have been to where I am taking you.

September 23rd

There is nothing you walk away from that I cannot restore, says the Father. Winning the upper hand through strife and contention only contaminates your soul and robs you of your peace. There is a storm on the horizon that can be avoided if you determine not to be pulled into its warfare and strife.

Fear not, says the Father. What can man do to you? What can man take from you that I cannot restore ten-fold? Let them have what they are willing to depart from love to attain. You cling to Me. Go low-- go low and worship. Humility is the secret weapon of the Kingdom. Going low will cause the assaults of the enemy and the plans of the dark one to pass you by (unable to attach to you).

You will find My blessing and My protection in the place of humility. In the place of humility you will be hidden in Me from the scourge of strife and debate.

September 24th

You are going to have to lift up your eyes to see what I have given you, says the Father. Your destiny will never be apparent as long as your attention is on the distractions of the enemy. Do you not understand that the dark one is all smoke and mirrors? He is like a toddler banging a pot with a spoon--he wants attention. He wants to see what he is doing in your life to register on your face. He wants to read his torment in your expression. Do you want to really upset him? Look in the mirror and say, "Bah ha ha!"

He that sits in the heavens shall laugh at the calamity the enemy threatens and at the strategies of hell against you. He shall laugh at the threats, torments, and trials. It chills the enemy to his core when you laugh the laugh of faith.

Nothing will separate you from My promises.
Nothing will rob you of your destiny.
Nothing will take you from My hand.

You are going to have to trust Me. You are going to have to laugh! You are going to have to let Me take it from here.

September 25th

I told you separation was coming, says the Father. This separation serves a purpose that you have actually prayed for (whether you realize it or not). Abram did not see the breadth of what I had given him until Lot departed. David did not inherit the throne until Jonathan was no longer at his side. Paul did not become the architect of what the church became until after Barnabas took John Mark and departed. The timetable for Jesus to ascend to the throne was not established until Judas betrayed him.

Your genius (that ability I have placed within you) will not thrive and come to fullness so long as you are surrounded by the relational distractions of unproductive friendships. There will be seasons of isolation. These are times that I am pouring Myself into you in a greater measure. I am a jealous God, and I am jealous over any influence in your life that draws your focus away from Me. Learn to be gracious and loving when friendships fade and camaraderie's cease. It is no one's fault. It is merely the voice of the bridegroom whispering sweetly in your ear, "Come away with Me, My beloved."

The intimacies of the bride and the bridegroom are not for the eyes of others, and the intimacy I am bringing to you in Me is not for public consumption or table-talk. The bride is about to meet her bridegroom in you. Prepare your heart. Adorn yourself with the wedding garment of worship and adoration. I will be known of you with a fresh and deepening way. You are about to come to know Me in ways you never thought possible. I cannot wait, says the Father.

September 26th

I want you to be an altar builder in this season, says the Father. It is a new day, and change is upon you. I am calling you to rethink your choices and tune your ear to My voice as never before. I have provided you with the oil of My Spirit to consecrate the altar of your worship. I have drawn you aside with Me and made Myself known to you. I am speaking to you from the burning bush with the voice of My commissioning.

The days of tending those few sheep in the wilderness are over. The hour of confronting the Pharaohs of the earth has arrived. The kingdoms of this world are become the kingdoms of your God and of His Christ! That Christ is within you, says the Father. He is not in you to suffer because the suffering of the Cross is complete. He is in you to be known and be made known in the earth. The message to the kings of the earth is to surrender or be overrun by the army of the Lord's host.

It is time to don the battle armor I have provided you and know that the victory is assured. This is what you have asked for and waited for, so hear My voice and obey it in the moment. You will see the enemy routed and the prey delivered from the mouth of the lion and the paw of the bear.

September 27th

As you go about your day, I want you to realize something, says the Father. Every place where you put your foot I have given to you. You are a principality in the earth. I will act and move according to your word in the lives of those around you and the places where you go. What are you going to do with that responsibility?

Your entire day will be a prayer walk. As you go, speak the thing desired, and I will act. I will tell you what I am doing in each household and each place of business. I want you to articulate back to Me in prayer what I show you saying, "Yes Father, your will be done."

I have placed you in your life like I placed Adam in the garden. You are to tend and to keep your environment. You are to subdue and take dominion over it. This honor I have given to you. This responsibility is yours. The angels stand ready to carry your prayer dispatches to the throne where they will be ratified for manifestation in your life and the lives of others.

Be bold to hear My voice, and be audacious in your prayers. Everything begins to change today, says the Father, as I activate My authority in your life.

September 28th

There is a battle ahead, but this battle is not an assault against you personally, says the Father. You will lead this battle in defense of others who are undeserving of the effort. They have placed themselves in harm's way through disobedience and lack of discernment. They are wondering what they will do now that they have found themselves in this mess. I have said I would send deliverers out of Zion. I am sending you into the situation with sword drawn and the angelic hosts at the ready to assist you.

You are to refrain from an "I told you so" attitude. The time will come for instruction and correction, but for now speak My word of deliverance and show the fierceness of My unconditional love. Do not listen to their protestations of what they say is the problem. You are not on their side--you are on the Lord's side. In this situation you are captain of the Lord's host.

Your friends will complain, "Why did you get involved in this?" You are to tell them, "If My Father got involved in sending His Son to solve my problem, what right do I have to withhold my time and resources from these undeserving people?" When the danger is past and the dust settles, says the Father, you will be tempted to "spank" them. They will actually invite you to sermonize to them. Refrain from this error. Simply pour in the oil and the wine and bind up their wounds and be on your way. This will stick with them for weeks and months and will ultimately lead them to surrendering their lives more fully to Me.

You are on a mission, says the Father. If you choose to accept it, you will be an emissary of My love, and you will gain yourself a promotion in My Kingdom. You have asked for promotion, and promotion has been promised. Promotion comes through exploits in a time of war, and this is an exploit to which you are well-equipped.

September 29th

I am going to bring some unlikely allies to your assistance, says the Father. I promised I would give you the riches of the heathen for your inheritance. I promised that kings would dangle your children on their knees. I am giving you favor with those you need to find favor with, and they will stand by you when others choose not to stand by you.

When these allies come to your aid, do not dismiss them or reject them because they do not belong in "polite Christian company." I am drawing them to you by My Spirit. I will acquaint them with who I am through you. The kingdoms of the world are becoming the kingdoms of God and Christ, says the Father. Those who populate those kingdoms and superintend those kingdoms are going to take on a new relationship with you. I am covering you with favor. They are going to say, "I don't know why I'm doing this, but I just want to help you." They will be blessed because they chose to be a blessing to you. They are going to be exposed to who I am because they chose to bless you.

You are going to be accused of being the friend of publicans and sinners, says the Father. Rejoice! You are in good company.

September 30th

These allies are going to know that I am your source, says the Father. They think you cannot make it without them. They think they are indispensable to your survival. They think you cannot prosper unless you are in their good graces. I am going to reveal to them the treasuries that I have stored up for you. I am the one in charge of the economies of the earth, and I will provision according to My good pleasure.

Even in his own arrogant opinion, no man will be able to say that he made you rich or that you need him to make it on the earth. You are in My employ, says the Father, and I will provision you from My favor and according to My good pleasure. I am not a miser counting My pennies and planning on just how impoverished you can live and still call Me Lord!

I became poor so that you can be rich. I suffered the lack of all things and was stripped of that which was rightfully mine so that you might live in houses you did not build and partake of vineyards you did not plant. I am foolishly fond of you. The biggest complaint of the onlookers will be that I have spoiled you with My goodness. Bah ha ha!

Fret not when the evil doers rage. Do not regard their words when they remind you of how much you need them. You only need one thing and one thing only--to sit at My feet and find your protection and preservation in the secret place of the Most High.

October 1st

Do not be afraid, says the Father. I will never leave you. I will never forsake you. There will never be a time that I will not provision you or protect you. You have been earmarked to receive the "exceeding blessing." There are no half measures in the Kingdom. What would you have me do for you?

Today I am acting in My sovereign grace to do for you what you cannot do for yourself. That is who I am and what I do. Put your trust in Me. Slow down, and wait upon Me in your situation. You cannot make things better in your own strength, but you can make them worse by acting in concert with the dark one's agenda for your life. He wants you to react in fear. He wants you to panic. He wants you to respond in anger and take your frustrations out on those around you. Be still and wait upon Me.

I am here, and I am closer than the breath of your nostrils. I am wrapping My arms around you and comforting you even now. Breathe in and breathe out. You are protected. I am acting on your behalf. I went to the Cross in order to be in your life and in your circumstance this very day and this very moment. Expect My delivering hand to be made manifest this day, says the Father.

October 2nd

The Father says today that there can be no compromise with the enemy of your soul. The concessions that the adversary is demanding will only be the beginning of his depredations into your life. He will not stop or relent until he takes everything near and dear to you. He is the destroyer of dreams that would devour all vision and hope. This will not stand. I will not tolerate anything less than total destruction of the strategy and plans of the enemy.

Do not compromise. Do not accept anything less than what I have promised you. You get to have it all, says the Father. This day I give to you your life, your goods, and your loved ones. I know that is not what you have been taught, but I say that there is not a person or a thread of cloth under your hand that will be left behind as a capitulation to the dark one. You get to have it all.

I made provision for all things that pertain to life and godliness. All means all, says the Father. Stop planning for the losses you think are on the morrow. Begin taking authority over the enemy and the thoughts of defeat and sorrow and loss that he is painting like an image before you. This is not My plan. Trust Me. Hear My voice. Act when I instruct you. Great will be your victory. Your reward is assured.

October 3rd

Trust Me to act in your life on My terms and in My timing, says the Father. I do not have any contingency plan for your life. I am not offering any consolation prizes for "Plan B." Do not rationalize away your blessing. I will never be late, and I will not arrive with partial answers or diluted solutions.

The enemy has predicted your failure because you are not perfect. He mocks your hopes because you failed to do everything right. I took the imperfection of your humanity into account when I crafted your destiny, says the Father. I do not look at performance. I am looking at a heart perfected under My hand.

Let the stress of the situation roll over on Me. Stress and pressure may tempt you to accept second best. You are not destined for disappointment or disillusionment. I am bringing the dreams of your inner man to the birth, says the Father. Work with Me by your faith. Cooperate with what I am doing. Harmonize your spirit with My sound that is sounding in authority on the inside of you. This is the hour, and this is the day and season of your deliverance. Trust Me, and step forward to your victory.

October 4th

You are hired, says the Father. You are hired to go into My vineyard. It will be obvious what to do when you get there. Leave your pruning hooks behind for I am the refiner and the perfecter of the branches. You are the reflection of My love and My undying fidelity.

I have indelibly inscribed upon your heart the maxim, "I am going to love you, and there is nothing you can do about it." Give love. Spend it lavishly on those who can least afford to repay. Pour out the love which cannot fail like an ointment of healing into the wounds of those who oppose themselves and oppose everything around them that they do not understand.

In the love that never fails, you enter the environment where failure cannot follow and even a dog cannot follow your trail. Are you exhausted with running from failure? Are you tired of trying to avoid disaster at every turn? Take a turn into My love. Open your arms and your heart, and allow My love to fill you with who I am because I am love. This is the "fail-safe" I have afforded all those who call upon My name.

I have nothing other than My love to give under any

circumstance, says the Father. I know that is not what you have been taught. Let who I am, however, speak louder than those who have nothing beyond a history lesson to give others as evidence of My existence. Give Me. Demonstrate Me. I will be on hand to freely certify My love with signs, miracles, and wonders.

October 5th

The Father says that the circumstances you find yourself in today are not permanent. Do not make plans based on current conditions. It is unnecessary to spend time figuring out how to work around what you think are your limitations. I am going to remove the limits that constrain you now and transition you to a new season.

If you make long-term decisions based on current challenges in your life, you will unnecessarily complicate the season of blessing that I am bringing you. It is a new day, says the Father. The pressure you are under is trampling out the vintage of a new day in which I will lead you in a new way. Do not retire or remove from the wine press you are in; it will not produce or yield sorrow but the joy of a new season and a transition to a greater measure of the things you have petitioned Me for in days past.

I will never forget what you have asked Me for, says the Father. I have noted every request and am acting now to bring about the desires of your heart that I have planted in you for this "now" time. Trust Me. Let Me take it from here.

October 6th

It is true that trusted friends have been few and far between, says the Father. The landscape of your life has been cluttered with the seeming wreckage of relational disillusionment. Have I not said that narrow is the way and few will find it? Why be surprised at the fact that you often do not have much company along the way.

Your friendships and relationships are subject to the arrangement of My hand for you are being set in the heavens in a particular arrangement to serve My peculiar purpose. Look through the earthly, and see the heavenly, says the Father. You are not as alone as it may seem from time to time.

As the stars in the heavens are so arranged for the navigational aid of men on the earth, so I have arranged the friendships and relationships of your life to guide you through the dark toward My greater purpose in the earth. Hold everything loosely. Love lavishly. Mourn not when change comes; rather, give thanks and sojourn on.

I am guiding you ever onward to the destiny I have crafted for you before the world began. It is there that the sons of God stand for joy before the foundation of the earth, and it is there that you are taking your place in the pantheon of My house forever.

October 7th

You believed Me, says the Father, therefore you get the reward no matter what. Believing for bigger dreams and greater accomplishments will warrant the same reward as actually going out and doing those things. Go ahead and dream. Go ahead and do exploits and scale the heights.

I rejoice when you dream the bigger dream! It is not a waste of time or an exercise in fantasy when you broaden your vision and dare to hope against hope for the extreme or unusual. What are you waiting for? Where your faith ventures, says the Father, your feet will follow! So, fear not and hesitate not. I love a dreamer. Dreams are the stuff that your tomorrows are made of. What you dare to believe for today you will be thanking Me for on the morrow.

This is the launching you have been asking Me for, says the Father, and the promise of a better day.

October 8th

It is a new day, and every new day is an opportunity for fresh sacrifice. Each fresh sacrifice is answered by fresh fire. There is nothing stale in your relationship with Me. There is no nostalgia in Me, says the Father, because I live in the eternal now. Do not look back. The past is a figment of memory stored in the tissues of your brain.

Set your affections on the now. You will then be livingly attached and connected to the vibrant breathing reality of who I am. The packets of grace and filaments of power that pulse from My character into your life course through the breadth and strength of your living connection to Me.

I am not the one that maintains and strengthens those conduits, says the Father. Your connection to Me is controlled, nurtured, and expanded by your time and attention not focused upon the world around you but upon the Kingdom within you. Look to that Kingdom, and it will produce righteousness joy and peace as the dividend of your passion for Me. This process is called, "putting on the mind of Christ."

October 9th

As you rise today, I want you to look in the mirror and inform yourself, "Today I will receive the kiss of the Father." This is the day that I will take you in My arms, fill you with My embrace, and give you the kiss of the son of My love.

The kiss of the Father is the kiss of My favor. The kiss of the Father is the kiss of My fondness which I will demonstrate in this 24-hour cycle. Look not on the morrow for this is the day I am demonstrating that I am foolishly fond over you. In My holy determination this day, I am making Myself known to you in favor, fondness, and the blessing of My good pleasure.

Rejoice, says the Father. You will spend this day in My embrace with My breath upon you, warming you and intoxicating you with My love.

October 10th

I am setting an open door before you today, says the Father. The only thing you need to do is walk through it. I have arranged the opportunities and prepared the way before you with favor and blessing. The angel of change is there waiting to initiate the change. When the moment comes, you will know it. Open your mouth and say what I tell you to say, and be silent when I signal you in the depths of your spirit to be silent.

I am your partner in life and in business, and I am not a silent partner, says the Father. I am ever there beside you--coaxing you and coaching you. I will bring you breakthrough. The breaker anointing is available. Receive it and activate it. Today is not a hard day or a hard season. Today is the day I demonstrate My authority in your life that comes and activates through yielded and audacious acts of faith.

October 11th

I have not restrained your blessing, says the Father. Depend on Me, and wait upon Me. When you find yourself in the gap between blessings, maintain intercession and trust. The world you walk around in all day is the staging ground for a cosmic conflict. The enemy wants to discourage you and diminish you. I have provided you with the protection and the weaponry of My Spirit to withstand the assaults of the evil one.

Today, says the Father, I would like you lean hard upon Me and allow Me to take the weight of the day from you and bring you through this harsh season. I will cause the rivers of living water in your belly to arise and wash you and cleanse the way between us. This day (this 24-hour cycle) was crafted ahead of time by My hand for your blessing. Look for that blessing and know that nothing shall separate you from My grace.

October 12th

I am your protection, says the Father. Your security is not in your situation. Your stability is not in your job. Your help does not come from the banker or the doctor or any human instrumentality. When all these fail you, I am the strength of your countenance and your high tower.

I have seated you in the heavens far above the din and despair of the challenges you face today. I have made you a principality in the earth and given you authority to speak in My name. I will be petitioned of you at My throne, and I will endorse the decrees you make upon the earth.

Your words have been stout, so let them be stout against your enemies. There is a shaking and an upheaval coming, and I have secured you so that there will be no loss. Look to My hand and My strong right arm. I will secure you and make your safety sure even this day, says the Father.

October 13th

I do not have any contingency plan for blessing you, says the Father, because it never occurred to Me that I could not pull off a plan. I am the Lord thy God. Is there anything too hard for Me? To seek to work around or devise some alternative plan that My promise will come to pass is to invite unnecessary complication.

I have said I would bless whatever you put into your hands. Be, therefore, discriminating about where you direct My blessing. Abram failed this test, and Ishmael was the result. Do you want an Ishmael on your hands? I did not think so!

Wait patiently upon Me, says the Father. I will close the gap between the promise and the blessing, and you will rejoice that while you were waiting and trusting you did nothing to complicate your life without cause. Trust Me. Let Me take it from here.

October 14th

My angel is standing by you this day, says the Father. The fountain of My refreshing is bubbling at your feet even now. The hand of man will not be your resource. I am your provider and your kind assistance at the hour of need.

The territory you find yourself in is unfamiliar to you but not to Me. I have directed many of My children through these seasons of challenge. They came forth shining as the sun, and you will come forth untarnished and unfazed. There is an hour ahead for you in which this looming difficulty will be but a footnote in the testimony in your life to My faithfulness.

I am arising in your circumstance today, says the Father. Look for Me in the challenge, and make room for Me to do for you what you cannot do for yourself. This is the hour I show Myself to be your strong defense and high tower.

October 15th

The wisdom of men pronounces what is, but the wisdom of God declares what will be. You have asked Me, "Father, what will be on the morrow?" My heart ached, says the Father, for the uncertainty I saw in your heart. I would give you to understand that the blood of the Cross was shed to remove every question and every doubt concerning My love toward you.

The Cross is heaven's "exclamation point" that answers with finality every question directed toward My loving character. I am willing, I am able, and I am acting on your behalf today, says the Father. No longer allow any questions of the mind to overrule the declarations of the Spirit.

I say again, says the Father, that no more shall you allow the questions of your mind to overrule the declarations of your Spirit! Your Spirit knows because it is the couch upon which I make My bed on the inside of you. Even though the winds blow and the waves crash on the ship of your life, My composure is undisturbed. Take your rest in Me. Take your solace in the strength of My countenance. I am your hope, and I will never die. Therefore, your hopes will never die.

October 16th

The Father says today that I formed the earth by the power of My word. The seas and the land sprang into existence at the words of My mouth. I have likewise placed My creative words in you that you might create and speak and know the power of My Spirit working in your behalf. So participate with Me this day in your own blessing. Open your mouth as you have watched Me do so many times.

Speak to the winds and the waves says the Father. Speak to the storm in your life. Come on! You can do this, says the Father. It is easy! Open your mouth and say what I say: "Peace be still!" And, the fun part is when you realize it actually happened. You will also notice you have arrived on the other side of the problem you have been trying to navigate.

Every father wants to see his children excel beyond what he has done. Have I not said in My Word, "Greater things than these shall ye do?" Now is the time (and this is the day) for that experience, says the Father. Listen to My voice, and follow My example. Do what you have seen Me do many times before. I will be there to back you up and bring it to pass.

October 17ᵗʰ

The Father says today to "resist not evil." Do you understand that I am your defender and protector? What can man do to you? What can man actually take from you? When you act in your own defense, you are deviating from My purposes for your life. It is My purpose in your life is to provision you and bring you via the shortest route to your greatest blessing.

The enemy knows where your panic button is and how to make you flinch. Lean on My grace, and you will prevail over the temptation to react with "fight or flight" when the enemy threatens you.

The threat is real, says the Father, but it is temporal. My protection is equally real but eternal. Lean on My grace. Trust in Me. Trust that I will show up in the conflict, rain down on you, and drive away every adversary.

October 18ᵗʰ

You are not out of time. Your life is not ruled by the hands of a clock. Your life is defined by My limitless power. Because I have time, says the Father, you have time. Do not allow the ticking of the clock to drown out My still small voice that is whispering to you in the winds of the day. My sound is reaching you. It is a sound that reverberates in eternity and carries you on the wind of its wings. I have put My sound within you, and it is going out into all your earth. My sound is causing all that I have placed under your hand to resonate in harmony with My promises.

People come and people go, says the Father. Situations change, and circumstances evolve to look very different from what you expected. Yet, My faithfulness remains. I am the constant (the constancy) in your life--constant love, constant provisioning, and constant protection.

You are not finite, says the Father, for I have made you to taste of My infinite nature. Be at rest in My infinity. What can man take away from that? Were you to give all your goods and all your relationships and all your energies to that, there would still be an untapped, immeasurable increase available to fill your entire life with My goodness and My blessings on your behalf.

Grieve not, says the Father. Fear not the seeming apparent loss. There is nothing man can take from you that I will not restore from My limitless supply. You are the provisioned one. You are provisioned from My storehouse, and I will not allow you to fall behind one wit of My fullness even today.

October 19th

The Father says today, "My son and My daughter, I am the God of "suddenly and exceedingly." I will come suddenly to your defense in this season. I will multiply you exceedingly in this season. I will come suddenly to your aid and bring My "exceedingly" with Me for I am not a hesitant God, and I am not an anemic God. When you are thirsting, I will not come to you with a dropper of water to cool your tongue. I will come with an ocean of refreshing and pour out upon you that which you cannot contain.

Avert your eyes My son and My daughter! Look not upon that which the enemy is doing for I am about to execrate the enemy from your life. The enemy has trifled with you and annoyed you and thought to distract you from that destiny which I am unfolding in this season. The enemy is going to experience the woodshed of God in this season. There is going to be a spanking because I chasten those I love when they set themselves in adversity against that which I am doing in the lives of My children.

The payoff is here, says the Father. It is not far off. I am provisioning you, so get out your checkbook and write the check! Today you will see a cloud the size of a man's hand. On the morrow the windows of heaven will open. I am a God of "suddenly and exceedingly!" Be encouraged this day. It is a new day, and it is a new season. Old things are passed, and new things have arrived. Rejoice!

October 20th

Fall on your face today, says the Father, for I would like to talk with you. This day you will walk among My declarations over you as a man walks among the trees of the woods. You are surrounded by My promise this day. You are walking under, over, and around My decrees. My words are taking root under your feet and raining down upon your head. My sound is drowning out the sound of the enemy. My sound is reshaping and remolding your past, your present, and your eternity.

Laugh at the enemy. Open your mouth as say, "Bah ha ha." The enemy is a child with a spoon beating on a pot. His earnest plan and purpose will not circumvent the protection of the Cross. The Cross is your defense, says the Father. The Cross is articulating itself in your situation and your circumstance. Go forth and conquer! It is a day of war--the spoil is yours, and the victory is assured.

October 21st

The Father says that My sound is reverberating through your life today. It is dislodging all things that are an offense to the Cross. This will change you, and it will change circumstances and situations that have become fixtures in your life.

You have petitioned Me for change. You have declared, decreed, petitioned, cajoled, begged, and bargained. I heard you the first time, says the Father. You do not have to keep asking Me about that issue in your life any longer. Enter into thankfulness for the finished work. Thankfulness for the finished work activates the high praises of God in your mouth. Let your mouth say, "Thank you Father for this deliverance you have brought into My life. I call it done now in Jesus name!"

High praise causes your Spirit to resonate in harmony with My sound. My sound is whirling on the breezes of your life to reshape and reform and even to restore. There is loss in your life that you have written off, says the Father, but I have not forgotten. I will not only restore the years but the blessings of those years as well. The season just ahead of you will be greater than the seasons behind you.

Your best days are ahead of you and not in your past. Take the rear view mirror and throw it out the window for there is nothing left to look back upon. Trust Me, says the Father. Have I ever really let you down? I will amend, I will bless, and when all things are settled, you will look back and exclaim, "Yes Father! Thank you. You do all things well!"

October 22nd

The time has been long, says the Father, and the questions many. The barnacles of a very human experience have attached themselves to your life in ways you thought they never would. You thought by the time you reached this point that things would look brighter and better. You wrongly concluded that you just expected too much and should have set your sights lower.

The variables of human experience have etched their own marks into your past and shaped you into a portrait of pathos and benign skepticism. I am about to change all that, says the Father. I am the God who makes all things new. I am forming a new you for this new season. It is a new day, says the Father.

You will no longer face the day with a tongue-in-cheek "wait and see" perspective. You will no longer shelter yourself with the pseudo-sophisticated, worldly-wise skepticism that finds its origins in the spirit of this world. To the world this attitude toward life looks sophisticated and suave, but from My perspective, says the Father, I see a gaping wound of unbelief.

I have unlimbered the wineskin of My healing ointments, and I am pouring in the vintages of restoration and hope. I am breathing into the dormant tissues of your optimism. I am holding your exhausted heart in My hands and massaging it back to a passionate, chest-pounding zeal.

This is what it means when I said your youth will be renewed like the eagles, says the Father. Even now you are going through the molting process in your memories and emotions. You are shedding the remembrances of former things. The harsh, emotional rigidity and sarcasm that has not served My purposes is being sloughed off and replaced with pink-soft sensitivity.

You are going to find tears on your cheeks more often in this season, says the Father. Let them wash away the disappointments of the past. Those tears are fortified with My forgiveness and strength. Forgive others. Forgive yourself. Let go and move on. It is a new day, says the Father, and I am gifting you with a new you, a new mind, and a new heart to serve Me in this new season.

October 23rd

The promises I made to Abraham are paying dividends in your life today, says the Father. The covenant which the man, Abram, and I ratified in the wilds of Canaan centuries ago reaches even now across time and culture to find a resting place in your life. That covenant migrated through the wilderness with Moses. It was consolidated on the Cross at Calvary. At Calvary the covenant gathered itself as a living thing around the man, Jesus, upon the Cross. The blood that spilled from His body redressed every covenant hindrance and impediment that would keep My promise to Abraham coming to fullness in your life today.

That promise is "on tap" in your life, says the Father--promises of destiny, provision, and protection. Your acts of faith activate that promise. Commit yourself to acts of daring. It is said that fortune favors the foolish, but I say to you that My favor fortunes the faithful.

The life of faithfulness I have called you to is not a pedantic, pastoral repose in the bounds of safety. I am calling you to so boldly step out that you lose all credibility with those that "seem to be such" on the mountain of religion. They add nothing to My Kingdom, and they will add nothing to you. It is true they are convinced that they hold the keys to your success. But I say to you, I am about to breathe on their paper kingdoms and clear the way for the assault of the kingdoms of the world by My generals and My mighty ones (whose number you are counted among). Gird thy sword upon thy hip, says the Father, for the fun is about to begin!

October 24th

I am changing your name today, says the Father, for I am changing your nature from one of deficiency to fullness in Me. I am extending Myself into you and drawing you up by ascension into Myself. You will no longer see limitation when you look within--you will see My Kingdom. You will no longer see vacancy for I am filling you with Myself and causing you to know Me with a greater degree of intimacy.

You were created to live and breath and walk in Me as I envelope and surround you with the warm embrace of who I am. You will never again be exposed or left helplessly open to the assaults of the enemy. The arrows that fly toward you will be deflected by Me for I am your armor and the shield round about you.

Repose in Me today. When the enemy threatens you, just choose to rest in knowing you are in My arms. He would have to get through Me to hurt you or take from you. Trust My grace to close down all the inroads of pain, lack, and conflict in your life. Peace is your portion today. Provision is on the way. Protection is yours this day by My hand.

October 25th

I am increasing you with My "muchness," says the Father. There is no void in Me. There is no deficiency or anemia in Me. My very nature is fullness, and out of that fullness I am stocking the shelves of your inner man from the inventories of My glory this day.

What do you need Me to be today, says the Father? Your greatest need defines who I am in you. My strength and My force is descending into the depths of your being. I have loosed the bowels of My compassion on your behalf. I am condescending into you that you might ascend into Me. I am bringing the "exceeding" of Myself over you with abundance to a great degree. I will eclipse the ravages of time and experience and cause you to shine with My glory and presence. Darkness and sighing will flee away. Laughter and joyfulness is coming.

What can man do to you? What can time, happenstance, or circumstance do to you when you are so overshadowed by My favor and provisioned from the treasuries of My abundance? Rejoice, says the Father, and trust Me. This is a day of challenge and a day in which I certify to you My carefulness over every minute aspect of your life.

October 26th

The Father says today to be circumcised in your heart. Only the circumcised in heart will find their place in the pavilion of My house. I have a seat for you here by Me, and no man shall usurp you from your place at My table. You do realize that you are a principality in the earth? Yes, it is true the enemy is thereabouts. How else would you know where to find the table I have prepared you?

Do not run from your enemies--do not run from the foe. In the presence of your enemies, you will find the provisions that the Blood of the Cross paid for in your life. See yourself seated with Me, says the Father. Do not look at what the adversary is doing. Look to Me and laugh. "Bah ha ha!" No weapon formed against you shall prosper. You shall condemn every tongue that rises up against you.

You bear My name, says the Father, and you were born for battle. The confrontation ahead will yield when you speak My name.

October 27th

The Father says today that you are not going to be able to solve the problem before you on the level of the problem. You are going to have to rethink your assumptions about what I will and will not do. The solution to the problem you are seeking will not be found in the playbook of the mind of man. Miracles are missed when you think you know what I will and will not do in a given situation. I do not think like a mere man, and I do not solve problems according to the dictates of man's expectations. I can do anything I want anytime I want, and I do not have to check with anyone.

Expect Me to show up today in unusual, unique, and unexpected ways. I am breaking down the barriers that have defined you and opening up new opportunities for new and greater blessings. Your life today will not look like it does a year from now. Even in six months, says the Father, you will look back and say, "I didn't expect that the Father would move that quickly in my life."

I am walking on the water toward you, says the Father. The storms and waves will not stop Me, and they will not stop you as long as you keep your eyes on Me.

October 28th

I am going to do for you what you cannot do for yourself, says the Father. I have no contingency plan other than launching you into your kingdom destiny. Your vision and your desire have been dismissed by many as fantasy. Do not listen to those voices. The voices of the critics and the naysayers do not carry the weight of My voice. Their voices have produced nothing but worthless chatter. They love the sound of their voices so much they cannot hear anything else.

My voice is the voice that created the heavens and the earth. My voice is the voice that spoke when you were wondrously formed in the womb of your mother. My voice is the voice that ignited the spark of life at the moment of your conception. I breathed My love and My promises into that preformed tissue and set you adrift within your mother's womb even as Moses was set adrift on the Nile. Moses found his destiny, and you will find yours, says the Father.

I am bestowing favor upon you this day. Cause your heart to

look up to Me and open wide like the mouth of a baby bird opening its mouth to the mother returning to the nest. I will fill you until you cannot contain any more blessing, says the Father. I know that this has not been your experience, and it is not what your teachers (in their religious wisdom) have taught you. They have a sparse god. They teach an anemic and a stingy god. I am none of those things, and in this season and beginning this day (afresh and anew), I will begin to show this to you in a new way.

October 29th

The angelic warriors are all around you, says the Father. Do not withdraw from the heat you feel today. The angels always show up in the heat of the day. This is a day of heat for you and a day of conquest. Do not retire from the heat. In the heat of the battle, you will find the angels at work. They were requisitioned by your prayers. You did not think I was not listening, did you?

The predator is the prey, says the Father, and you are a principality in your life. Even as Abraham negotiated with Me over the fate of Sodom, so you have power and authority to negotiate the destiny of those I have put in your hand. I will be petitioned of you, says the Father. I will speak with you as a friend to a friend for I am your covenant partner. I have covenanted with you to possess your possessions and drive out the usurper.

This is the season of strategy and the season of tactical advance into enemy territory. When the enemy sees you coming, he will think he has you where he wants you. What he does not see is the phalanx of angelic shock troops that will be on hand to crush the opposition!

October 30th

I know what it is to have tears on My face, says the Father. On the earth I knew strong crying and tears as I walked out My passion among those that neither understood nor perceived who I was or what I was called to do. I am imparting to you My passion. The fire in My loins is becoming the fire in your belly.

Because of the intensity I am imparting, you will find that you will no longer be welcome in polite company. They will say, "It will never do to have such a one at our social functions. They will ruin it for everyone!" They will complain, "All they do is talk about God!"

I will have you show up without invitation, of course, because I never observed the social niceties and neither will you. You will walk in their midst, and they will "take knowledge of you that you have been with Jesus." Your face will shine as Stephen's face the day he came to Me. You will be asked to leave, and you will reply, "Bah ha ha!"

My fear will be upon them as you speak. Signs and wonders will precede you before you arrive and continue after you are gone. Because of the angel activity in your life, they will say your house is haunted. They will come with TV cameras--the cameras will not work, and the sound equipment will fail. In frustration they will realize that they will not be able to cash in on what is going on around you and turn to leave, but I will arrest them, says the Father, for they will (with surprise) take note that what they saw taking place in you is now on the inside of them. They will run to you for help, and you will laugh the laugh that issues from the throne.

I will deliver them, and I will change them. Your community will be skewed on its axis as they suddenly realize that the Kingdom of God showed up, and they have a decision to make. Help them make the right decision, says the Father, for this is what it means to win cities and not just individuals for God!

October 31st

I am right here beside you, says the Father. I will never leave you, and I will never forsake you. I am closer to you than your next breath. I am closer to you than your own hands and feet. Open a door and I am there. Turn around and you will bump into Me. I am in your space. You are in My lap. My arms are wrapped protectively around you this day.

Breathe deeply of who I am in your life today. Allow who I am to reach saturation in your life in this 24-hour period. Was I not good to you yesterday? I will even show you My goodness today. It is all the same to Me, says the Father. You wake up in a new world every day, but I never sleep and never change My mind regarding My love for you.

Trust Me. Trust Me. Trust Me. It is a new day and a new season. Drink deeply from the fountain of My faithfulness in your life today.

November 1st

I am changing the way that church gets done in the earth. I am laying the hand of My emphasis on "being the church" instead of just "doing church." You will no longer simply go to church in this hour, says the Father. From this day forth you will stand up and be the church in the earth.

The primary difference, says the Father, is that the demonic realm is going to stand up and take notice. The demonic minions are going to be called in on their day off. Because you are taking your position in the Kingdom, the principalities and powers will no longer get to sleep in on Sundays. The demons and powers of spiritual darkness are going to a seven-day work week and doing extra shifts, says the Father. They are going to have to set their alarms earlier and cancel their dinner plans because they will be working late. The church in the earth is going to plague the domain of darkness and rob its inventories and release the captives.

I am going to change nations in a day, says the Father, because My church is taking their position in the earth. The pundits and media demagogues are going to rush through makeup to report breaking news as I redraw the geopolitical map of the earth in a day. So, man your battle stations and sound general quarters for the day of the advancement of My Kingdom has arrived, and there will be no more delay. The time for trifling with the affairs of this life is over. The distractions that you have allowed to occupy you are over.

This is a day and a season of change and transformation, and you are called to take your part and claim the spoil. You will not wait until afterward to wear the garland of victory. You will wear the epaulets of victory going into the battle for the outcome is assured. This is the time you have prayed and longed for; therefore, rejoice and let the energy of My Spirit invigorate you. This is the time of My glory, and you get to be a central participant in the process!

November 2nd

The Father says that you are one who loves deeply and commits strongly. This gets you into trouble occasionally and leaves you vulnerable to a spirit of rejection. I am healing you on the inside from that rejected spirit. Self-pity and despondency will lift off of you today.

I took all the hurts and rejection and the contempt of men upon Myself on the Cross. I was rejected and despised that you might be accepted and honored before the Father which is in heaven. No longer will you seek the honor that comes only from men. I will content you with the honor that comes from the throne.

Do not be troubled when you are despised of men. When men despise you on the earth, the angels applaud you in the heavens. When friends and family abandon you on the earth, angels rally around you in the heavens. You are mine, says the Father, and not one hair shall fall from your head without My full and complete attention.

You are as the pupil of My eye, says the Father. You are not insignificant or unnecessary. Others think they can live without you, but that is not the sentiment of heaven. I am not willing for My plan to move forward without your involvement. Come up to Me, says the Father. Ascend into Me as I descend unto you, and we will rejoice together and find the destiny that has been encoded in your spirit since before the foundation of the world.

November 3rd

There is no shelf life to my promises. My promises to you have no expiration date. Your faith, however, can be fatigued. Your trust in Me can falter. Feed your faith, says the Father. I gave you a portion of My faith at the moment of your conception. It is a portion equivalent to that which is needed to move every mountain and conquer every obstacle you will face in your lifetime. When you were conceived, I measured the challenges you would face during your life and accorded you the measure of faith equal to the challenge. You have on the inside of you (from birth) the resources from the Throne that are necessary to put you over in life and bring you through every trial.

Stop looking up and stop looking outward for your answers. Did I not say, "The Kingdom of God is within you?" Trust and rely on what I put on the inside of you. True dependence on Me, says the Father, is not an outward reaching but an inward leaning on who I am on the inside of you.

You are equipped by My hand for the current task. Now go out and be "God" in the situation even as I made Moses "God" to Pharaoh. Your adversaries will perish in the waters of deliverance that I am sending just as Pharaoh perished when Moses stepped out in reliance upon Me.

November 4th

Look around you, says the Father, and all you see is dust and ashes. You wonder how I am going to get you out of this one. Take heart. At least you have not lost the confidence that I can deliver you. I certify to you this day that I am your deliverer and your strong and present help.

Do not look to man. What man can give you that he can also take away? I am bringing into your life a deliverance from on high that does not originate with man and cannot be taken away by man's machinations and deceptions. They will scratch their heads and wonder how you did it. They will wonder how you "got away" with this because they will not see My hand at work. They confine their concepts of Me and their opinions of what I will and will not do inside a narrow little box that is far from My presence.

I refuse to work within the parameters that religious minds set for Me, says the Father. Let your eyes be drawn away from the pundits and opinion-makers, and cast your full confidence in Me. When the smoke clears and the dust settles, they will look to you for an explanation. Your answer will be brief and enigmatic for them.

November 5th

If you say it, says the Father, I will do it! If you will not say it, then I will not do the thing you desire. I have laid the credibility of My promises upon the line in My Word. I am calling upon you to lay your credibility on the line and believe that I will not allow one of your words to fall to the ground.

Have you sought Me for My plan for the season ahead? Have I not spoken to you in the night seasons? Have I not opened the vistas of your mind to see the tableau of glory I am bringing to bear in the earth?

Open your mouth wide, says the Father, and I will make your mouth and your heart and your mind a conduit through which the vision of "My Kingdom come" will be articulated in your life. This is not the hour for the timid or faint of heart. Gird yourself with courage, and gird your thigh with the boldness of one who knows his God!

November 6th

I am not going to get angry, says the Father. Go ahead and ask Me the thing you have hesitated to ask. You assumed that I would not hear and would not hearken. You assumed I would be displeased that you would make such an audacious request. If you had looked at My face when you first dreamed it up, says the Father, you would have seen the pleasure in My eyes and the smile on My face. Have you not heard the whisper in the night, "The Father loves a dreamer?"

The angels assigned to you have long been impatient with your dishwater prayers. The angels assigned to you were created for audacious exploits of world-shaking power. Go ahead and ask of Me, says the Father.

Let us put the angelic resources at your disposal to work and to see what a difference they will make in your life and in the earth. Your loved ones languish in despair and suffer under the heel of the enemy. Your community is held in the grip of the principalities and powers in high places. Your prayers are the key, and you are going to have to ask me, says the Father. Deliverance is on your lips for yourself and others. Open your mouth, and let fly the glory!

November 7th

Is it time for your ship to come in, says the Father? Is the next business deal the one that makes all the difference? Is it time for the Iraqi Dinar to RV? Will the next lottery ticket be the winning one? What are you waiting for, says the Father? If you knew the gift of God and one that speaks to you in the night season, you would speak the "words of life" and would provision spring spontaneously from the nothingness and bareness of your own life.

Now is the day of salvation. Do not wait for another day. Now is the time to move forward in faith. Now is the time to act and obey and speak the delivering word for I am with you. You need not wait on the chronicles, the right time, or the right place. I am with you--act now!

I can deal with anything but your refusal to make a bold decision, says the Father. Do not fear making a mistake for I will make even your mistakes to prosper you more than all of the wisdom found on Wall Street or in the halls of the governments of the earth. My Kingdom is coming in power and purpose and provision, and it is coming in and through you! Now is the day and now is the time for you to act boldly!

November 8th

Strongholds do not come down without effort, says the Father. When the children of Israel invaded the Promised Land, I did not drive out the giants all at once. The strongholds in your life will not yield simply because you want them to yield. They will not fall merely because you ask Me for that outcome. Yes, I will answer you, but the answer I give presumes that you are a necessary part of the process.

You are intended to be a participant in every victory that you win. I am a God of power and action, and you (as one of My children) are called to continual campaigns of spiritual conquest. There are enemies before you that will become permanent fixtures in your life if you understand that I have armed you and equipped you for their removal.

Allow Me to teach your hands to war and your fingers to fight. The weapons I will train you to use are mighty, and they will pull down the obstacles and impediments in your path. You have asked Me for answers and a destiny that only lies on the other side of conquest. So, when warfare is the natural result of those petitions, do not complain. I will be with you every step of the way, and I will sustain and maintain your cause as you come along beside Me. We will stand shoulder to shoulder and armor to armor in the ranks as we go forth together.

As you enter into the conflict, know that the outcome is assured. You are going forth this day to win the prize you have asked for--to conquer the enemy of those you have petitioned Me for and to conquer the enemy of your soul.

November 9th

The Father says today, "Make up your mind who will be going with you into this next season." You are in a time of transition, and in six months things will not look like they do today. This is a season of change as I am lowering My arm to the earth to do battle with those who have sought to contravene My purposes in your life.

The onslaught is beginning, and there will be casualties. Name those you are not willing to write off, says the Father. I will count them your friends and preserve, protect, and strongly defend them. The community you are in and the circles you move in are going to face a shift in the axis that have defined them and given them security. Your security is in Me, in hearing My voice, and in doing what I tell you to when I tell you to do it.

There will be those who will follow you because you have named their names before My throne. There will be others who will follow you because they realize that I am on your side, and there are those that connect with you that are left standing at the end of the day. Call those names, says the Father, and the angelic hosts will be dispatched to be a rear guard to those you lift up before Me in this time of challenge and victory.

November 10th

The Father says today that your supply is established by the economy of the Kingdom of God and not the wealth or resources of the earth. Your access to the resources of heaven is determined by acts of faith and daring.

Did I not say to the rich young ruler, "Sell all that you have and distribute unto the poor, and you will have treasure in heaven?" This was not a call to impoverishment, says the Father. This was an opportunity to access heaven's inventories that are available to every believer--you as well!

Are you ready to close the disparity gap between your experience of limitation and the unbounded supply available to you in the heavens? You are going to have to listen to Me. You are going to have to trust Me. You are going to have to do what I tell you when I tell you, and the windows of heaven will open. The economy of the Kingdom will be visited upon you on the earth.

I made Abraham rich through the promises I made to him. You are an heir of that promise, says the Father, through the blood of the Cross. Do you honestly think I have any interest in your living in poverty? Did I not say that I became poor so that you could be rich? Supply is at hand. Your obedience activates the stores in the heavens and releases them to you upon the earth. This is the path of progress and the opening of the windows of heaven!

November 11th

The Father says today that angels are accompanying your steps. You have met them and were not aware of them. They are running interference against those that are wearying themselves to assault and defeat you. My plans for your life cannot be controverted (changed) by storm or trial or economy downturns or any other thing. My chosen destiny for your life cannot be derailed or diverted.

As your decrees arise from your lips, the angels are laying your petitions before the throne of My mercy. Mercy is the mandate that governs all My dealings with you. Your experience of that mercy will increase as you show mercy to others. Set a guard on your mouth today for the angels are near, and they act and react according to the words of your mouth.

Open your eyes My child and see the host of those that are working for you. There are more for you than there are against you. Trusting in Me will assure the outcome. Let your trust be in Me. Hear My voice. Do not commit to the plan; commit to Me. You thought you knew the plan, but you did not know it with the clarity that I know it. Follow Me, and let your idea of what should happen go by the wayside. I will not let you slip or falter. I will deposit you on the banks of safety and take you onto your next assignment in My Kingdom.

November 12th

Let your prayer today be, "Father, make your arm bare and show your might in my situation today." I am the God who does not negotiate with the enemy, says the Father. I am the God who crushes the opposition. I am moving today in your physical body to bring health and healing as you cry out to Me.

The effectiveness of the stripes of the Cross is manifesting in your organs and in your bloodstream, says the Father. No more will exhaustion and sickness plague you. No more will you wonder, "Are my years shortened?" I am renewing your youth, bringing physical transformation and restoration. Even in areas where you made choices that hurt your health and damaged your body, I am releasing forgiveness and rolling back the ravages that have torn you and harmed you.

I am giving you grace to change and be changed into a new person with new habits and activities this day for I would that you live long and walk long in My Kingdom on the earth, says the Father. I have much for you to do, and I will not allow your years to be shortened. Hear My voice, do what I tell you, and the strength of your youth will be renewed. You will run with the footmen and outstrip the horsemen and know the vitality and strength of My resurrection life.

November 13th

The Father says today that I am speaking to you through dreams, visions, and portents. I will not leave you without guidance and direction in this season. I am bringing My Word to life more and more as you seek My face and desire to know what is on the morrow. Without first revealing My plan in ways that encourage you to walk in cooperation with that plan, I will do nothing.

Let your eyes be open and your ears be attentive, says the Father. No more wondering what is going on around you for I am not leaving you in the dark. Hearken to My voice and articulate what you hear to those who will not otherwise listen. There are those around you who are flailing about for clarity and understanding. Let your voice be heard as you put on My mind and put off the mind of the world.

The world does not know Me, and it is not going to understand you. They will estrange you and ostracize you because you do not respond to their efforts to control and contain you. I will cause you to break out of every containment wall they erect to isolate and quarantine you, says the Father. My Kingdom in you cannot be held back or suppressed.

Hearken to My voice, and let your voice be heard. When they turn a deaf ear, simply move on knowing you have done what was your duty. They will experience the woodshed of God when they could have known divine provision and protection even in this season. Your responsibility is to follow Me and relinquish the outcome, says the Father.

November 14th

The Father says to not look back. Yesterday's manna will not sustain you today. Yesterday's vision only speaks of the past and not your future. Your past will not define your future, and present circumstances are not commentary on what tomorrow holds. I am the one who holds tomorrow in My hand, and I will shape your life and your circumstances according to My plans and purposes.

My character is so broad and so deep, says the Father, that every morning is a new opportunity to learn things about Me that you never knew or conceived. Relinquish the past. Let go of the emotional attachments to the people, places, and things that (at present) have no active role in your life. I will hold them in My care. You put your attention on Me and My plan for your life. I will keep safe that which you have committed to My care.

Do not look back, says the Father. I am the God of the "now." Yesterday is gone, and tomorrow is a probability that will not unfold in the manner in which you might think. This day is your assignment, and this day is where you will find the packet of grace that I am unfolding on your behalf.

November 15th

There is no temptation befallen you, says the Father, except that which is common to man. I am the uncommon solution to what you are facing today. I am your peace--I am Jehovah-Shalom. I will never leave you; therefore, your peace will never leave you. I am Jehovah-Jireh; therefore, your provision will never leave you. For all those things that I am to you, I can never be separated from you.

You can never be separated from your provision for I am your provider.

You can never be separated from your peace for I am your peace.

You can never be separated from your health for I am the Lord your God that heals you.

This is the banner that I am raising over your life today, says the Father. It is the banner of My indissoluble fidelity toward you. Who I am in your life today supersedes the circumstances of the day. Look for My faithfulness to show up and be strong in your life today.

November 16th

The Father says today that I do not build with hewn stones, and I do not make cookie-cutter Christians. The sound of men's tools hammering on My children is an offense to Me, says the Father. When I formed and fashioned you, I did not use a blueprint and a slide rule! I formed you in a womb and conceived you in the loins of your parents. You are unique, and I take umbrage at those who seek to mar that uniqueness by stamping you with their image.

You are made in My image, says the Father, and it is My image that I want you to reflect and not the image of man or the stamp of man's character or personality. The alignment I am calling you to is alignment with My purposes and conformity to the mandates of My Kingdom in your life. I am setting you in the ranks of My army, and you will find that I have placed you in a circle of My choosing.

There are those who will ask you, "Why are you keeping company with those people?" You do not get to choose who I place with you on the front lines. Unlimber your thinking from all bondage to the good opinions of men, says the Father, for I have not called you to conform to man's ideas but to My revelatory truth.

I am calling you up to the heights in Me and to let your feet be like hind's feet on the lofty peaks of My purposes in the earth.

November 17th

I am reproducing Myself in you, says the Father. You have My eyes; you have My mind; and, I am producing My heart on the inside of you. You have My image indelibly etched in your spirit, soul, and body. I have imparted to you My nature not to fail! No longer will there only be a superficial experience on your part of the depth of My person and My presence. My "deep" is calling you into the trackless expanses of who I am on the inside of you. There is so much more than you have tasted thus far, says the Father.

Come away My beloved. Let go of the boundaries of the familiar and the shallow, no longer requesting license of the guardians of the status quo for their permission to lose yourself in Me. My words are bounding you and buoying you out beyond the breakers and reefs of religion to set your chart across the billows and waves of the intimate experience in who I am on the inside of you.

November 18th

I am going to show the world what My church looks like in the wild, says the Father. The four walls of religion are being obliterated in human culture. The ghetto of religion will no longer imprison My people. I am raising up lion-like warriors, who are breaking out of the limitations of culture and religion. They will show what My church is capable of when released into its native habitat.

Nations will tremble and political systems will reel as the world realizes they can no longer contain or restrain My sons and My daughters. Sound the advance, says the Father. It is time to go forward and seize the prey from the mouth of the lion and the paw of the bear. I have heard the cries of the miserable and the bound. I have heard the cries of those languishing in poverty and sickness. I have heard the cries in the night of those who are perishing, says the Father.

The hills will melt and the mountains will flow down as I descend into My people in a fresh, new manifestation of power and deliverance. You are My instrumentality, says the Father. Let you mouth speak My verities. Let your hand be the first hand to touch the sick. Let your hearts be the first responders to the destitute and the naked.

I am about to turn the societies of men on their axis and bring their focus riveting on My occupying force of sons and daughter who have determined to maintain no other fidelity than to My name and to My Kingdom!

November 19th

There is a sound of war in your life today. The enemy thought he could asphyxiate you under the suffocating cloak of religion. He dared to approach you with his predations. My wrath is aroused, says the Father. My anger now burns white hot against the principalities and powers who presumed they could extinguish My testimony in your life-- this will not stand! I will destroy the destroyer in your life.

Rise up and shake off the burdensome discouragements of the day, says the Father. Your future is not determined by the pundits or by the leading economic indicators in the global economy. I am provisioning you through a currency that cannot be manipulated. It is the currency of My Kingdom, and I declare that you are now delivered from the chains of limitation and impoverishment.

Go forward today and lavish yourself upon those who can least afford to repay you. Lavish them with My love because love is who I am. Luxuriate the disenfranchised with My care and My favor. As you do for others what they cannot do for themselves, I will do for you what you cannot do for yourself.

Your breakthrough is at hand, and your season is now, says the Father, to know the destiny that I brought you into the earth to establish!

November 20th

What possessed the enemy to think I would stand idly by while he dared to trifle with you? Watch and see as I strike the earth with My fist and drive off the dark one who dared target you with his assaults. Behold and wonder, says the Father. Have you ever imagined you would see fear in the eye of a serpent?

I am unwinding the coils of the enemy that have encompassed you, says the Father. You are going to breathe easier. Where there has been restriction, there will now be enlargement. Where there has been heaviness and hands that hang down, you will now soar into the heavens upon wings of expectation.

I am establishing over you the solidity of My faithfulness and fidelity. Come running to Me, says the Father. I am the open door where you will find refuge. You will shelter between My knees as you behold the destruction of the strategies and tactics of the enemy in your life. You have waited a long time for this day, says the Father.

November 21st

Do not look for pennies from heaven, says the Father. I am not that stingy. I do not put My hand over the coffers of heaven when you approach My throne. In the moment you ask of Me that which is needed and necessary to your life, My hand has already moved to pour out a blessing that you cannot contain.

The hour has come when supply will no longer be a distraction to you, says the Father. I will manifest the manna from heaven that meets your need just as I manifested the manna from heaven that fed the multitudes in the wilderness. I am that manna, says the Father, and I can no more withhold any good thing from you than I could withhold Myself from you.

I know that is not what you have been taught. They have claimed I cherish some "higher purpose" in denying and withholding My stated promises from your life. Who are they anyway? Did they give their sons to meet your need? How dare the sons of men presume upon the generosity of My hand.

Open your mouth wide, says the Father. I am about to give you a full heart and a satisfied belly. You will have enough to meet your need and plenty left to provision those who look only to you for sustenance. Open your hand to the poor, and I will open My hand expansively to you. I am banking My glories in your life for you are My chosen conduit of blessing into the earth.

November 22nd

I am going to show you the difference between credibility and anointing, says the Father. You have been told you must be aligned with men if you hope to fulfill your destiny. You have been required to associate yourself with the tents of the movers and the shakers on the mountain of religion. It did not sit right with you when you heard this because My Spirit was recoiling from the manipulation and religious politics you saw taking place.

Why seek the honor that comes from man rather than the honor that comes from God only? I have not called you to be cannon fodder for the wars that men fight against each other in the competition of religion. I have called you away to seek My face and know what it is to experience My hand on your life.

I have not touched you because you were honorable or qualified, says the Father. I have anointed you because they did not think I would; I am a sovereign God. I can do anything I want anytime I want, and I do not have to check with anyone!

Fill your horn with the oil of My Spirit, says the Father. I will cause you to be a tree full of the sap of My presence and rooted in the favor of My throne. It is a new experience, says the Father. I am drawing you away with Me that you might pour out of who I am to those who least expect to see Me move in your life.

November 23rd

I have called you to be a "son of fresh oil," says the Father. It is time for you to empty that which came forth out of yesteryear's oil press. There are fresh olives waiting to be pressed into fresh oil in your life. Empty your horn of that which sufficed yesterday. I will fill you with oil that will break the yoke of bondage today.

The oil that I give, says the Father, only lights the path ahead of you. There is no anointing in Me for turning back or retreating from the battle. Be moistened in your spirit man this day with the fresh oil from the anointed ones that stand before the Lord of the whole earth.

You have felt the piercing and wondered what was taking place, but I was only making accommodation for pouring into you what you have been crying out to receive. You said in your heart you would not be satisfied with anything less than the original extract of who I am, says the Father. Even this day that is what I am dousing you with from head to toe!

Go forth and rejoice, says the Father! It is an "oil of joy" and an "oil of healing and deliverance" over every malady and oppression of the enemy.

November 24th

Receive the medicinal remediation I am applying to your heart and soul even now. I am restoring you and renewing you for My purpose and My pleasure, says the Father. They think they have left you behind, but when they get where they are going, they will find that I translated you there ahead of them.

Do not be dismayed, and do not be angry. If they could have done differently, they would have. Just know that I have called you to make a different choice with those I put across your path. Say in your heart, "No one is disposable!" Yes, says the Father, one man's trash is another man's treasure, and I am making you My trash collector as I demonstrate the fullness of My unconditional love in the earth.

November 25th

The angels are vying for an opportunity to get in on My plan for your life, says the Father. You represent a plum assignment in the angelic realm! By your faith-filled prayers, you have requisitioned a small war in the heavens. The angels love to spill the blood of My enemies, and they are whetting their swords and anointing their shields in anticipation.

Fret not about the timing of things for the rumbling of chariots draws near to you this day. The fierceness of the war cry of angels is splitting the air around you, and tentacles of Jezebel are trembling for she knows she has no more time left to work her sickness in your life.

Victory is yours, says the Father. Rejoice and know that I am the one who always causes you to triumph through your confidence in Me!

November 26th

I am the God of battles, says the Father. It is who I am, and it is what I do. It is not possible that you would go without the protection of My hand. There is no assault of hell or onslaught of the enemy that can prevail against you. I have surrounded you with My person and vouchsafed you in My everlasting arms.

Though I be ancient of days, says the Father, My eye is not dim nor My arm weakened that I cannot save you this day. Put your confidence in Me. Ask Me! Ask Me that thing you desire, and see if I will not melt the heavens and come down in response to your cry.

I delight in harboring My children safe from harm. I delight in blessing those to whom you petition Me, says the Father. So call their names--the names of your children, your loved ones, and even those around you in the community--and see if I will not demonstrate My pleasure to save, heal, and deliver.

November 27th

I am pouring out My Spirit upon you as gentle rain and warm honey. Taste My sweetness, says the Father. Taste and know the fury of My love for you. My love for you spans eternity and reaches to unfathomable depths. There is nothing of Myself that My love will withhold, says the Father. Receive it! Breathe it in! Embrace all that I choose to shower upon you today.

You are the beloved. Between us, eternity embraces finite humanity and is fulfilled in love and fullness of blessing and intimacy. Come away, My beloved, and be lost in My love for you even this day, says the Father.

November 28th

Have you considered translation as a form of transportation, says the Father? You have already experienced it and were unaware of it. In fact, I have done many miracles in your life that have gone unnoticed by you or anyone else. I do not sound a horn or make a special announcement every time I show up in your life.

Cease asking, "Where are the miracles?" I daily laden you with the miraculous and the unusual and the unique, says the Father. Let your hearts cry be, "Lord, open my eyes to see what you are doing today!"

Let your heart's cry be, "Lord, let me participate with you in the miraculous today!" I would that you be a participator and a conduit of divine intervention in your situations. Stop looking up as though I have not showed up yet! Step forward and act, and I will come through for you and for all those that you stand for this day, says the Father.

November 29th

Hear My voice in your life today, says the Father. My voice conveys the substance of My Kingdom. My voice breaks the assault of the enemy against your life. My Kingdom comes to you by means of My voice. I have given you a hearing ear to receive your deliverance as a package from heaven. I am releasing My sound in your situation today by virtue of My voice that is powerful and articulate. Hear My voice today and respond.

I have given you the ability to hear and to speak. What you hear from My throne you are commissioned to speak in the earth. What I have said regarding your life becomes substance in the earth as you open your mouth and release what you hear Me saying. You are the conduit of My voice, and My voice is the means of your deliverance and blessing. Open your mouth, says the Father, to allow My sound to issue forth.

My sound is breaking over the situations and circumstances you have been petitioning Me for, says the Father. Allow My sound to be voiced in the earth today. My sound is signaling you. My sound is amplified in your ear and broadcast in your mouth. My sound is drowning out the sound of the enemy and the whisper of the accuser. Even this day, says the Father, determine in your heart to be the conduit of My sound into the earth, and you will see the victory you seek made manifest.

November 30th

The Father says today that the bleak outlook you see before you does not reflect reality in Me. The circumstances you face did not catch

Me by surprise. I am not sitting astride the throne of heaven wringing My hands and wondering what I am going to do next. Let your trust and your expectation be upon Me like never before.

I will be found faithful in your life. I will not leave you, and I will not forsake you. My promises are not being put to the test or strained by the rigors of life in your situation. Let your rest be in who I am and what I have promised. Even today, says the Father, put your confidence in Me and know that I am working to will and to do My good pleasure on your behalf. This is the day and the 24-hour period that I turn things around and bring you to victory.

December 1st

I will never leave you without counsel regarding your life, says the Father. I speak to you in dreams; I speak to you in visions; and, I speak to you in a thousand ways throughout your day about the myriads of issues that affect you (both great and small). My thoughts toward you are not general or vague. My thoughts toward you number more than the sands on all the beaches of the world. My thoughts toward you number more than the stars in the cosmos.

In all of this, says the Father, there is not one sentiment found regarding you that falls outside of love. It is true there are times you do not feel My love toward you. Move toward the flame. Hearken to the intuitive voice of My Spirit inside you. Move toward the warmth of My love, and you will find yourself at My feet for love is who I am and not just what I do.

Hearken to your dreams. Write your dreams down. Dreams are the flash cards of the soul. I send these images to you nightly. Dreams are the hieroglyphs of My Spirit. I put the spirit of inquiry inside of you that you might decipher their meaning and find meaning and direction in life. Do not be as the fool who ignores and passes on to his destruction.

Dreams are the "magnetic-resonance scan of the Great Physician," revealing slice by slice the minute images of things that influence and affect your life in the unseen realm of the Spirit. Your mind does not often comprehend or even remember your dreams which are why you must go to My Spirit for interpretation. In so doing you will find answers that you seek for things that are pressuring you.

Your destiny is not far off, says the Father. Your destiny is wrapped around you each night as a comforting blanket. I nurse you each night in your dreams. I breast feed you the milk of destiny to give you hope and expectation of great promise. Be not discouraged--trust. Trust Me and listen to Me and seek Me for understanding of things you do not comprehend. You will ascend into Me, says the Father, and you will take on My image and My character. You are more than a conqueror, so rejoice as I show you the battle plans of the day.

December 2nd

The Father says today that I am bringing you out of darkness and confusion. I am bringing you clarity and understanding. The question marks in your life are going to come into sharp focus, and you are going to see through the fog of unknowing. Do not be surprised or shocked by what is revealed, says the Father. Your first reaction will be to act without thinking to correct things. The Father says to you,"Wait on Me."

Wait upon the prompting of My Spirit. I am going to teach you to live with imperfection. You are going to learn that My grace and favor and promises were not made on the condition that you do everything right. The fulfillment of your destiny is not predicated on you becoming some inhuman example of infallibility. Every promise I have made and every dream I have given you takes into consideration your shortcomings and outright failures.

Even in the midst of your flawed humanity, you will find My favor! I am foolishly fond of you, says the Father. I love you unconditionally, and yes, there are many things in your life that test My resolve to do just that. I am pouring Myself into you and surrounding you with favor as with a shield. I am buttressing and protecting you by clothing you with Myself. I am not concerned you will not grow out of the things in your nature that do not reflect My character.

Relax into Me, says the Father. Rest in who I am in you. Turn your face to Me, and allow the transformation to take place. Do not worry about whether I will reject or deny you. The only thing that can separate you from My care is your determination to distance yourself from who I am in your life. Content yourself with My love, and trust that I have all in hand. The only preoccupation you need this day is to love Me and know that you are loved in return with an everlasting love.

December 3rd

I have an account to settle with you, says the Father. Your faith has made a demand upon the resources of heaven. Your hopes and dreams have generated a demand upon the inventories in glory. Your desires and aspirations have tugged upon My heart of compassion.

I am a just and a righteous God, and I always settle My honest debts. Through Calvary I made it possible for you to obligate Me by your faith. I delight to see you taking full advantage of what I died to make available. The angels in heaven shake with anticipation and excitement when the aroma of your faith reaches the ramparts of the throne.

Go ahead, says the Father. See if you can bankrupt heaven. Spend your faith--spend it lavishly! Luxuriate in the measureless faith I have accorded you. This is not Wall Street. You cannot tap or diminish the resources of the Throne! Let your requests be audacious and bold. I will not rebuke you or chastise you for I delight when you feel just how far I am willing to go to bless you.

Today is the day that you can turn things around by your faith. Go ahead. What are you waiting for?

December 4th

Do not borrow your dreams from someone else's life, says the Father. Out of love and mercy, I will bring those efforts to failure every time. You are unique. You have a destiny. You are a world changer and a Kingdom warrior. Walk in the destiny that I have hewn out for you before the foundation of the world.

Your destiny does not use anyone else's life as a template, says the Father. You will often walk after your own destiny in a state of unknowing. It is not important for you to understand or comprehend. Simply obey, and put your foot forward. I will enlarge your steps and bring you to the purposes I have ordained for you.

I have called you to place your dependency on Me today, says the Father. Many times man's ideas and the guidance of others only reflect their lack of faith in what I can and will do in your life. Move beyond those limits. Hear My voice as I speak to you softly in the silence between the words of others. I am drawing you out of the company of men into My presence, says the Father. Have you not been wondering what was wrong when you gathered in their midst?

Allow My voice to lead you and guide you until you have fully donned My person as the garment of My Kingdom purpose for your life.

December 5th

I will make you laugh, says the Father, and all that hear you will laugh with you. Though your vision seems like it is barren and that it has lost its young, I will bring it to fruition and fulfillment.

I am the Lord your God. Is there anything too hard for Me? Have I not spoken? You are going to have to make up your mind, says the Father. Either you heard Me or you did not hear me. Either I gave you a confirmed promise or you were just wishing. Have I not undeniably and unequivocally verified My promises to you?

When you believe what I have said, you are not merely putting your confidence in the prophet. You are putting your confidence in the God who spoke through human instrumentality to provoke your faith and raise your hopes aloft. Trust Me, says the Father. Know that I am with you this day to raise you up and lift you into the heavens, where all things are possible in Me.

December 6th

You are going to hear Me call your name today, says the Father.

Your response in that moment will make all the difference in what I am doing in your life in this season. Today, the opportunity is put before you to shorten the waiting for the answer you have been seeking. Yes, the waiting has been long , and you have wondered if I was even listening to the urgency of your cry.

Understand that answered prayer is determined as much by whether or not you are listening as by whether or not I am listening. Are you listening, says the Father? My sound is coming into your life in this season. You are going to hear Me call your name at the appointed hour. Your response to that call will make all the difference.

December 7th

I have dipped My quill into the ink of My limitlessness, says the Father. I am scribing your destiny on the leaves of your heart. There are no limits in Me for I am the "Boundless One." It is My nature and My character to remove the limitations that you face. Do you realize that you are My habitation in the earth? Where you go today, I go with you. What you face, I face with you. What you endure, I likewise endure.

From within you I send the resonance of My presence into every setting you enter. Whether it is the public square, your school, or your workplace, I am there. When I sense resistance (whether it is resistance to you or resistance to My Spirit), it is My autonomic response to push back and to overcome. I do not have to stop and think about it, and I do not have to pause and gather My strength. Those who sin against you sin against Me. Those who resist you resist Me. I will respond in My strength through your weakness.

Expect Me to get a little testy with your adversaries today, says the Father. I do not take kindly to those influences and elements in your life that contradict the provisions of the Cross. I am pushing back the boundaries and expanding your territory. Rejoice, says the Father, for I am working with you to will and to do My good pleasure.

December 8th

The barrier you face today will be overcome, says the Father.

Draw upon who I am on the inside of you. I am your sufficiency. There is no external dependency that will serve you in this hour. It is time to gain your self-sufficiency in Me. It is now that you must rid yourself of every debilitating outward dependency.

Did I not say that "Christ in you" is your hope of Glory? There are many that prattle on with claims of anointing and power. You will know them by their focus. Are they saying, "Come here" or "Go there?" Listen to the voice of My Spirit as I affirm once again that the Kingdom of God is within you.

Loosing yourself from external dependency is the definition of maturity in My Kingdom. You will not hear this from the gatekeepers of religious credibility, says the Father. They need to hold you in thrall to their agenda, but My Kingdom within you will not be bound and will not be limited to what takes place inside "the box." The hour is come and now is that I will spill you out into the world. I will take the bushel basket of religious limitation off of you so that you might shine and make manifest My glory to those that languish in darkness.

It is a new day, says the Father. Yesterday's thinking no longer serves My Kingdom purpose. Take on My mind and My passion this day, and you will find yourself in the very center of My plan for your life.

December 9th

As I called Abraham out of Ur of the Chaldees, so I have called you out of the mountain of religion. You are stepping out of religion into demonstration. Today (in this season), I am activating the demonstration of the Spirit in your life. Step out of religious expression into that demonstration of My Spirit. You will no longer talk about Me; you will demonstrate Me to others. I will go with you, and I will work with you to expose the world to who I am in the "now."

Your best days are ahead of you because My best days are ahead of Me. Yes, Moses parted the Red Sea and Elijah went up in a flaming fire. Yes, Enoch walked with Me, and I took him. Yes, David slew the giant, and Samson carried away the gates of the enemy. Those mighty feats are but footnotes to what I am doing in the earth even this day, says the Father. I am sending anointings into the earth that will command nations and shake the kingdoms of the world to their foundations. You are eligible to receive these mantles as you draw yourself away with Me and to My sound that is reverberating throughout all the earth.

Can you hear My sound, says the Father? It is a sound of war and a sound of the prey snatched from the mouth of the lion and the paw of the bear. I am standing up in the earth with Davidic fury to wreak righteousness and establish justice. I am standing up in the earth to overthrow principalities and subdue powers under Me, and you get to participate as you hear My voice and harmonize your spirit with My sound that is going out into all the earth.

Receive My sound within yourself, says the Father. Stand upright upon thy feet. I will talk with you, and My words will change, transform, and renew you to My purposes. Your problems and challenges are the small dust on the balance, says the Father. I am weighing nations in the scales of My purpose in this hour, and I will bring forth justice unto righteousness and cause you to know the fulfillment of every promise I have made in your life.

December 10th

The Father says today that you are "Elohim" among the Elohim. Did I not say that I was the first-born of many brethren? Being born into My Kingdom is not a matter of reckoning--it is a matter of reality. My DNA pulses in the very depths of your spirit. The character of My Lordship, says the Father, strains in the traces of your humanity, longing to burst the bonds of limitation and bring victory and conquest to the enemy of your soul.

The blood of Christ shed on the Cross made you a mighty prince in the earth, says the Father. In the eternities I dandled you on My knees and regaled you with tales of your own life yet to be written. Did you ever wonder when I put the "measure of faith" in you? It was not a clinical procedure. It was a passionate Father imparting something of Himself to a supplicating son and daughter.

Stand up on your feet today, and grasp the scepter of authority purchased for you on Calvary. Declare the efficacy of the blood of Christ over every area of need in your life and the lives of others. The hour has come, says the Father, to snatch the prey from the predator of souls and establish My Kingdom upon the earth (upon your earth) even this day.

December 11th

Allow My grace to conform and transform you this day, says the Father. Allow My cleansing influence to wash you of all worldly contamination. I am here to change and cleanse. I am here to mollify the wounds and soothe the scars of bitter past experiences. It is a new day, and I make you into a new creature that you might walk before Me and be perfect. Accept that perfection as a cloak of favor in My presence. Allow My presence to wash and renew you today.

This is the unconditional love wherein I love you. This is the transformative influence by which I change and renew you even in the season and this day, says the Father.

December 12th

Humility is your greatest ally in spiritual warfare, says the Father. I exalt the humble in their time of challenge, but I set My forces in array against the proud and stubborn of heart. Do you understand what humility is? Humility is the response of your heart to who I am in the situation you are facing. Do you honestly think taking matters into your own hands will produce anything positive?

Relinquish the outcome, says the Father. You cannot fix the problem. Let Me take it from here. I am the God who is more than enough! Guess what? I do not need your help. Put your trust in Me today to provide for you and to provision you for tomorrow. I will calm the storm on the outside, says the Father. You must calm the storm on the inside.

Rest in Me today. Do what you can with what you have, and trust Me to make up the difference. Trust Me to make good on My promises. I will not fail, and I do not falter. This is the day and the 24-

hour period when I will prove that to you. So, go ahead and thank Me. Go ahead and seek the Kingdom. Go ahead and laugh the laugh of faith for the "check" is already written, and the answers you seek have already been discharged from the heavens.

December 13th

The ground under your feet is not your stability, says the Father. I am your assurance and your firm foundation--not your job, your 401k, your possessions, or your relationships. When all of these fail you, I am still Jehovah-Jireh, your Provider. If all of these things would be taken from you, My mercies would yet be renewed every morning.

I will never leave you; I will never forsake you; and, I will never cease to be who I am in the midst of you. The mountains tremble and the nations shake, yet My Kingdom is unfailing and unshaken. Do you know where My Kingdom is, says the Father? It is not in a building or found in a pew. My Kingdom is on the inside of you, and it is lending itself to your life every day. My Kingdom is extending its strength, life, and vitality to everything you touch.

Trust in what I have put on the inside of you this day, says the Father. Allow My Kingdom to have the ascendency on the inside of you. Let My Kingdom govern your words. Let your attachments be to My Kingdom and not to any other created thing. You will then know fullness of righteousness, fullness of peace, and fullness of joy.

December 14th

You are a sojourner in this life, says the Father, but you are not a transient. As I gave Abraham a sure inheritance in the land, I will give you a resting place. When I walked as a man, I had nowhere to lay My head. I did this as an act of vicarious suffering so that you might be sure and secure in the land where I might send you.

I am your security, says the Father. Your security is not in the banker or the lending institutions of this day. I am shaking the economies of the earth even as I shook the ancient land of Egypt. It is time to let My people go. I am raising up deliverers and demonstrators of authority and power who will walk through life independent of the chains that greed has formed in the hearts of men.

Even as I sustained hundreds of thousands with manna every morning and water from the rock, I will sustain you. Men can lock their treasures away in steel vaults and, yea, find a myriad of ways to oppress the poor and afflict My people, but I will sustain you and be your provisioner. I am not limited by the vagaries of a modern economy, says the Father. Put your confidence in Me, and hear My voice for I will cause you to sow in this land and be recompensed.

December 15th

The Father says today that I will bless you with long life. You will be well-stricken in age; the years will be good years worth living and worth remembering. Your natural strength will not abate, and your eye will not grow dim. You will dandle your children's children upon your knees and will leave an inheritance to your children.

As Jacob, you will bless your sons, and leaning upon your staff you will worship Me. Your gray hairs will be a crown of glory, and I will cause the princes of the earth to bow down to you as a son to a father he loves. You will be gathered to your fathers in a good old age, and your later years will not be years stricken with sickness or feebleness.

You will not be feeble of mind or feeble in body. I will feed you with My vitality and strength. When sickness comes, you will rise up and declare the words of this promise, and I will prove Myself to be the unfailing God who does not fail to make good on My promises. I will not put on you the diseases that ravage the populations of the earth. Your health will be atypically strong, and the medical community will marvel and wonder at your stamina and clarity of mind.

I will provision you for the years, says the Father. I will move your enemies far off from you and surround you with favor as with a shield. I will give you sons and daughters and will restore to you the ravages of brokenness and rejection. I will make even your enemies to be at peace with you, or they will experience the woodshed of God.

As I have said, I will render to you a hundred-fold in the earth. Look not on the instability of the earth, says the Father. Consider not the experience of others but rather the faithfulness of My Word. I am encoding My DNA and the genome of My substance into your physical body and your mind and your spirit. You will not fail in old age and will rule as a principality and a power in the earth to the end of your days.

December 16h

I am not an ungenerous God, says the Father. I am willing to spend Myself on your need today. What is your heart's cry this day? You are going to have to ask Me. Your asking, says the Father, is the preamble to receiving. When Abraham asked for a son, I gave him many sons. Why would I do that? I am the "more than you can ask or think God."

If you can "think it," then you have not yet explored the bounds of My willingness on your behalf. If you have "asked it," then you have not comprehended the fullness of My magnanimity toward you. My name is not Jehovah stingy, says the Father! I am not reluctant to answer, therefore, do not be reluctant to ask.

Being who I am and knowing what I know, it is My great thrill to watch you explore the boundlessness of My love for you. As you come to know My love, you come to know Me for love is who I am and who I will be in your life even this day.

December 17th

The Father says today that you must learn to leave the details to Me. Abraham of old tried to work out in his mind how I would give him a son. He thought he was too old. He thought I would make the son of his steward his heir. He only considered his limitations and not My unlimited ability. The result was Ishmael. You must leave the details of how I will answer you to Me.

Much unanswered prayer arises from thinking you know how I am going to act and what I am going to do in any given situation. I am not inscrutable in the area of answered prayer, says the Father. Have I not said, "More than you can ask or think?" Take your eyes off the process and keep them upon Me. There is no variableness nor shadow of turning in My promise.

You can rely on Me; therefore, you can pray the end result with confident expectation that I do all things well. I will always act in accordance with My promises, says the Father, for that is the primary reason I left you the Scriptures. I want you to know what to expect in life. I know that men try to explain away situations where it seems I did not follow through. Not only are they not coming up with the right answers, they are not even asking the right questions. Put your confidence in Me, says the Father. I will provide; I will deliver; and, I will make good on My promises in your life.

December 18th

I will be entreated of you, says the Father. What I birth on the inside of you will result in struggle within you even this day. It is not comfortable, but it is necessary. The lesser destinies of your past are struggling against My best and My highest will for your life. My blessings are not bestowed upon your strengths, says the Father, but rather upon your weaknesses. Your weaknesses are the substance of the incense of yourself that is offered to Me by the angels upon the golden censor in My presence. It is in your weakness that I glory! It is in My strength that you will find My faithfulness.

I have not called you to the possible, says the Father. I have called you to the impossible. It is only through the impossible that you enter into an understanding of My plan and how I think when I look upon human weakness. I only think in terms of what men consider miraculous. I am not capable of mendacity, and I do not "do" average, says the Father. Do not settle for second best. Do not offend the testimony of My love for you by asking for "less than" or merely "good enough."

It is time to believe Me and ask Me for that which only I can accomplish. You have hesitated to petition Me because you did not want to be disappointed. The Father says, "Bah, ha, ha!" You do not have any clue what I am about to do. I am about to do exceedingly abundantly more than you can ask for or think, says the Father. Are you ready?

December 19th

The Father says today that I am bringing a militant love into your heart in this season. As you look into the hearts of loved ones in the coming days, you will see much barrenness. I am activating an entreaty within you to bring these people afresh and anew before My throne. I will not leave your loved ones in the chains of emptiness. As you demonstrate My love and as you demonstrate who I am to them, you will be planting an incorruptible seed that will come to fruition.

In the Scriptures did I not promise Cornelius that I would bring salvation to his whole house? The enemy exerts his greatest efforts against the family because the family is the only framework for human relationships that predated the fall of Adam. I am redeeming families in this season, says the Father. Not just individuals but whole families are being visited by the angels of change who are sent with a commission to initiate the change that delivers from the power of the evil one.

Open your heart, says the Father, before you open your mouth. Even to those who despise and hurt and disregard you, allow My militant love to flow unconditionally. Speak with your heart to your loved ones, "I love you because I love you, and there is nothing you can do about it." Out of that love I will demonstrate Myself, and you will see My hand moving strongly to deliver your family and loved ones even in this season.

December 20th

The Father says, I am the God who gives exceedingly and abundantly more than you can ask or think. Cry aloud, and spare not in your request and petition. I do not answer your need on a minimal basis. I do not give sparingly. Abundance is the base line for all that I do in your life. Let your capacity to receive from My hand be enlarged and increased even this day.

Yes, I am the "more abundantly" God, and that truth is shining through in spite of centuries of misinformation disseminated by small minds declaring the contrary. I love expansively and give expansively. I do not just give of My substance, says the Father, but I give of Myself. This day you will find Me among the gifts that I give.

Lack is ending in your life. Bid farewell to sorrow and sighing for it shall flee away in the aftermath of the breakthrough I am bringing to your life. Breathe in and breathe out of My Spirit, says the Father. Let the totality of who I am and what I am doing in you take root this day and establish the deliverance I have promised.

December 21st

There is no going back, says the Father. The people, situations, and circumstances of the past are a figment of memory that cannot be reconstituted. Put your hand to the plow, and do not look back. The Kingdom of God is before you and not behind you. My promises are part of your future and not part of something that has passed.

That which is familiar is an intoxicating influence, says the Father. Things that are known quantities can become a false security that will only comfort you for a short time. Allow Me to be your Comforter. Allow Me to be your security and your assurance for the days ahead. We are going into unfamiliar territory. This is necessary because you have asked Me for an uncommon blessing.

If you want things to be different, you must abandon the past and embrace change. Change is the banner that has been raised over your life in this season. The angel of change has come to initiate the change that will break the shackles from your life and lead you to the center of My will in this day and this hour.

December 22nd

There is going to be a wedding, says the Father. The bride and the bridegroom will rejoice together. The wine of My Spirit will flow freely. The table of provision is now laden with every good thing. The celebration is all in order. The angels stand about with bated breath awaiting the first guests to arrive.

The bridegroom is seated in the anteroom of heaven reflecting on the season of His betrothal now coming to its conclusion at last--a life of service, a death, and a resurrection. I have waited a long time for this hour, says the Father. My sons and my daughters will at last be united! Sorrow and sighing shall flee away. The laughter of children will fill the earth. Humanity and divinity will now enjoy unfettered intimacy.

You have an honored place in the nuptial celebration, says the Father. Oh, My people, the gown is prepared and the attendants wait to adorn you with connubial glory. The bridegroom whispers, "Come away with Me, My beloved!"

Are you ready, asks the Father? The musicians have begun to play. It is time! Take My hand in this hour, says the Father. It is time to make our way down the aisle to the consummation of all things spoken by the prophets.

December 23rd

In the coming year, says the Father, I am going to show you where to find the hundred-fold return. You will have an opportunity to invest your life, your time, and your resources into My Kingdom in a bold way. It will be a new field of endeavor and will not have the trappings of success in evidence. It will be a bare field. But as you plant your faith and pour yourself out like a drink offering, I will cause it to produce and bring fruit in the Kingdom and blessing into your own life as well. Do not expect the crowds to come flocking around to admire the results, says the Father. I have reserved this blessing for you in a time of famine. This increase is just for you.

Be prepared for a shift, and be listening for My voice to bring the command, "Get ye hence." I have poured into you My glory and prepared you for an endeavor of boldness and faith. I will cause you to do exploits in My name in this season as you hear, as you obey, and as you believe Me for the uncommon results that are possible when you trust My leading and My directions in your life.

December 24th

The Father says today that I will act in your life because of the Son and not any other thing. I will take action in your life in answer to your prayers and petitions because of the Cross and not any other thing. I take no other inventory than the tally of what was paid for on the Cross, says the Father. It is because of what Jesus, My Son, died for and who He is that I will move heaven and earth today to meet your need.

The enemy would have you disqualify yourself from My grace. He would tell you that you are not worthy. He would say that you are not good enough. He would say you have not measured up, and therefore, your prayers must go unanswered. I say to you, declares the Father, that the Cross is the only measurement I take to determine your eligibility for answered prayer. The Cross of Christ establishes your entitlement to My mercy.

Lean into Me this day, says the Father. Lean into My blood-bought entitlement. Do not look to what you have or have not done or at your own worthiness. You cannot earn My favor. You cannot be good enough for what is freely and unconditionally given. I am your righteousness, says the Father. I am the "all" in your all even this day and in this season. Cast aside every false weight and every false measure. A false measure is an abomination to Me. The only scales of justice that I accept are the scales tipped by the Cross of Christ.

Trust Me, says the Father, and expect from Me this day. Reach out for My unconditional grace. Stop trying to talk Me into giving what I have freely and unconditionally bestowed upon you. The hour has come for you to inherit all that I have provided. Accept it. Believe it. Walk into your day expecting it. You are the favored son of the Monarch of heaven. Your victory is assured.

December 25th

You have asked what is coming in the new year, says the Father. I say to you that of My government and of My peace there shall be no end. Nations will rise, and nations will fall. I fold them up as a blanket and put them away for the day to come. My Kingdom is the constant in your life and not any other thing.

Changes ahead will not reflect one iota of deviation from My faithfulness in your life. You will cry out to Me, and I will answer. You will call to Me, and I will say, "Here I am." Fret not for tomorrow. I am sufficient for the challenges of tomorrow; therefore, you are sufficient for the challenges of tomorrow. Weep not for the losses of the fading year. Let not thoughts of sorrow or sighing enter into your mind or lodge in your heart. Rather, rejoice for the season ahead and know that My righteousness and My faithfulness will be your vanguard and your strength for every challenge.

December 26th

The Father says today that breakthrough comes through actual change and not through year-end resolutions. My anointing is upon what you do and not what you merely resolve to do. Resolutions are external and dependent on a self-imposed expectation. The grace to change draws upon the internal grace of My Kingdom. Change prepares the way of the Lord and makes straight My approach to your life.

You have said you want something different in the coming year, says the Father. You can have breakthrough, however, things are the way they are because of what you are doing. If you want something different, you must draw up the power of change from the well of salvation I have placed within you.

Fear not, says the Father. Instability and the unknown are the first two ingredients I use in the recipe for a miracle. I am inviting you to walk in the miraculous and see breakthrough in the coming year. Will you return the RSVP and walk with Me on the billows of change and breakthrough, or will you delay another year?

December 27th

I have not called you to limitation, says the Father, and neither will you be destined to live out a spiritually anemic existence. When you call, I will answer. I will answer your petitions with an outstretched arm and a mighty hand. Let your voice be heard today, and I will make My arm bare in response to your cry.

This day your faith and My fidelity will come together and reshape your future. Do not look to the things that are behind you and consider not the former days. Consider this--I am a faithful and loving Father who will establish your goings and raise you up to new heights in Me in the coming season. Do not despise the promise, says the Father, for it was purchased by the shed blood of Christ. Rather, know that He is faithful that made the promise, and He will perform it.

I will roll back the years of devastation and disappointment. I will restore that which you thought was irretrievable. I will fulfill My promises in your life in this season, says the Father, and you will laugh the laugh of faith as you see the whitened harvests become bread on your table and victory in your life.

December 28th

The Father says today that I have you tucked away in My heart. I have hidden you in the cleft of the rock until this storm is past. The threats and vulnerabilities that loom before you this day will pass, but My strength and My faithfulness will remain to all generations. Victory is not just a word in My vocabulary, says the Father. Victory is My bond and your assurance from My hand.

As you have trusted Me in times past, so trust Me now. Trust Me to be who I am, and trust Me to do what I do. I am not capable of standing idly by while you struggle and suffer. My hand is available. Let your mouth pray this day, and your petitions will activate My strength and My deliverance in your situation.

Never allow your mind to convince you that I am a passive God, who sits back and observes the problems of life and does nothing. That is not who I am. Remember the Cross--it is the sure expression of My willingness to act. The resurrection speaks of My ability to deliver on every promise. It is a new day, says the Father. Old things are passing away, and all things are becoming new. Get your feet shod with My word of promise This new day calls for you to walk in a new way and trust Me in a greater dimension for greater miracles than you have seen thus far.

December 29th

The Father says today that the enemy is going to offer you a compromise. He is going to suggest that you settle for second best. He is going pressure you to "leave well-enough alone." It is going to seem logical and appeal to your peace-loving nature. But the Father says to remember that I am a God of war and that I did not come to bring peace but a sword into this conflict.

I am placing it into your heart to accept nothing less than total annihilation of the works of darkness in your life. Every captive will be set free. Every stronghold will be brought down. Not one idol will be left standing. I am placing a warring spirit within you, says the Father, to fully come into the possessions I have given you and leave not one place in your life for the enemy to lurk and peep and mutter.

Remember this: Though the enemy has said you will not survive and do not have what it takes, I am your sufficiency, and it is My right arm that is bared in your life in this season. I am making your forehead like flint, and I am causing your hand to cleave to the sword until every victory is won, every prayer is answered, and there is nothing left of the enemy's activity in your life.

You get to have it all, says the Father. Do not accept the compromise solutions of the enemy of your soul.

December 30th

Make My presence your priority in life, says the Father. You have asked what would bring My greater blessing to your life, and I say, "Come near to Me in worship." As you go low and worship, you will find that My presence dissolves the mire and contamination of the world that plagues you at times. My presence brings the refreshing that you seek and the joy that you need. In My presence you will find the fullness of joy, fullness of peace, and fullness of blessing.

Seek My face, and you will see My hand. I am not sleeping, and I am not occupied elsewhere. I see what is on the morrow and what you are facing. Seek My face, says the Father. Seek Me early and often. Let praise be continually in your mouth. Refuse to give the enemy and the problems of life your precious attention. I will guide you and direct you as needed. I will not leave you without a pathway through the circumstances you are facing today.

Come and sit at My feet as did Mary, Lazarus' sister. I love to spend time with you. I love to encourage and wash you with My presence. This is the purpose for which you were created and where you will find your greatest purpose.

December 31st

The Father says today that the coming year will be a season of contrasts in your life. You will see the great darkness that will cast many around you into consternation. You will walk in the light of the morning spread on the mountains and know that I have apportioned you favor from the throne. A thousand shall fall at your right hand and ten thousand at your left hand, but you will be safe in My pavilion.

I will answer questions that you have asked for some time, says the Father. The answers I give will bring greater questions. The implications of the lessons I am teaching you at this time will cause you to lose all confidence in the arm of flesh. In the year ahead your dependence will be completely upon Me as I take you into uncharted territory.

I know the way through the wilderness, says the Father. All you have to do is follow Me. Your mind will rebel at times but be prepared to still your mind and follow the guidance of My Spirit. You can get to where you want to go, but you are going to have to relinquish your hold on the familiar and only draw your security from My presence.

Are you ready for adventure? Are you ready for change? Change is necessary, and change is possible; however, you are going to have to draw yourself away with Me and follow My voice through the days ahead.

ABOUT THE AUTHOR

Russell Walden is an author and speaker with decades of experience in both traditional pulpit ministry and in the business world as an entrepreneur in the IT sector. In 2007 along with his wife Kitty they founded Father's Heart Ministry (www.fathersheartministry.net). They travel the United States and abroad teaching and mentoring in the prophetic. Russ and Kitty have prophesied to thousands who by their own testimony attest that their lives have been transformed by the unique and positive character of this man and woman of God.

Made in the USA
Middletown, DE
08 February 2015